(a treasured Bk of Reminders)
that

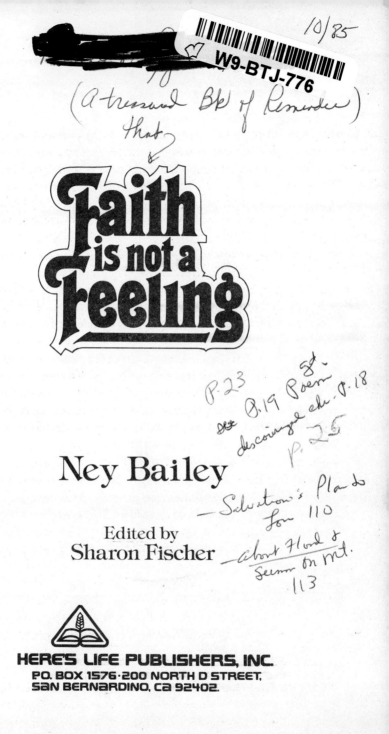

Faith is not a feeling

P.23
see P.19 St.
Poem
discouraged chp. P.18
P. 25

Ney Bailey

— Salvation's Plan do
Lou 110

Edited by
Sharon Fischer
about Flood &
Sermon on Mt.
113

HERE'S LIFE PUBLISHERS, INC.
P.O. BOX 1576·200 NORTH D STREET,
SAN BERNARDINO, Ca 92402.

ISBN 0-918956-45-5   HLP: 95-00-22

Unless otherwise identified, Scripture quotations are from the New American Standard Bible, Copyright © The Lockman Foundation 1960, 1962, 1963, 1968, 1971, 1973, 1975, and are used by permission.

Scripture quotations identified KJV are from the King James Version of the Bible.

Scripture quotations marked LB are taken from *The Living Bible* (Wheaton, Illinois: Tyndale House Publishers, 1971) and are used by permission.

Here's Life Publishers, Inc.
P. O. Box 1576
San Bernardino, CA 92402

Acknowledgements

It is with the deepest appreciation and heartfelt gratitude that I acknowledge:

My family—especially my parents, and Brenda, Edwin and Kim—for their reading and giving suggestions on portions of the manuscript.

Mary Graham—who has lived with me during my labors and has demonstrated great love and patience. I have appreciated her honesty and her constructive suggestions. She should receive special recognition for being a discerning sounding board who has counseled me wisely and has given valuable editorial assistance.

Sharon Fischer—who, as my editor, has given me excellent advice and suggestions. She has had a way of asking the right questions to draw out more detail and of helping to make my material more readable. She gave of her time and of herself. She has become more to me than an editor—she has become my friend.

Janet Kobobel—who did final editing; Judy Downs Douglass, editor of *Worldwide Challenge* magazine; and the Campus Crusade for Christ publications staff for their encouragement and hard work. They are a great team.

Frank Allnutt—for his confidence in me and for overseeing the publication of this book.

Bill and Vonette Bright—for allowing me to join the staff of Campus Crusade in the early years when there were only 100 of us, for being an example to all of us to believe God for great things, and for providing spiritual food and an atmosphere of love and acceptance, so that I could begin to grow up in Christ while on staff.

Jean Pietsch Prensner—for helping to recall some of the incidents we shared in our years together.

David A. Sunde—my colleague and dear friend who agreed to read the manuscript "slowly, carefully and purposefully" for theological accuracy. I am grateful for his encouragement and for his investment of time on my behalf.

Sallie Clingman—my long-time friend who has taught me many things about the Lord and who was the one God used to name this book.

Don and Sally Meredith—for their valuable input into my life in the area of relationships.

Hav and Dotty Larson—for the privilege of living in their summer home at Lake Arrowhead, California for the last five years. The quiet, restful retreat atmosphere, the view of the lake, the birds, squirrels and tall pine trees have made it the perfect place to write.

Carol Rhoad—our dear secretary and friend who was the first to help me in the typing of material for the book. The last day we spent together is where this book begins . . .

It is with deep appreciation and a grateful heart
that I dedicate this book to my father and mother,

ED AND ALBERTA BAILEY

who have loved me and given themselves sacrificially to me.

Foreword

I first met Ney Bailey in 1961 when she left her native Louisiana and her profession as an adoption caseworker to join the staff of Campus Crusade for Christ. In the ensuing 17 years she has served on our campus staff at the University of Arizona, initiated and directed our personnel department and helped to pioneer a pre-marriage and family emphasis within our movement. In addition she has been one of our national representatives since 1969, traveling and ministering to our staff and women in the United States. Ney has made a vital contribution to this ministry, with her habitual attitude of "What can I do to help make things better?"

Everywhere Ney goes she gives two things: her heart and her knowledge of God's Word. The biblical principles she shares are grounded in personal experience, and there is ample proof that they can change lives.

I often hear the positive results of Ney's ministry; thus, I was personally delighted when I learned that she was writing a book. *Faith Is Not a Feeling* provides solid scriptural teaching on the life of faith. Having seen the impact which walking by faith has made in my own life and ministry, I see the need for a book such as this.

Our feelings and God's Word do not always coincide. Ney gives insight into why this is so and how the conflict can be resolved. She gives very practical help and input no matter where one may be on his pilgrimage with the Lord.

This is a very personal, interesting and fast-moving book. It combines tragedy, humor and drama in a way that holds the reader's interest. I predict that you will want to read and reread this book and recommend it to others. I highly commend it to you.

Bill Bright
President and Founder
Campus Crusade for Christ

Preface

"What would you do if you only had a year to live?" asked my director, Paul Eshleman, to a group of us in a staff meeting.

I thought, "I would try to put into print some of the things I have been speaking on because they seem to be ministering so powerfully in people's lives." Soon after that, Judy Downs Douglass, of Campus Crusade's publications department, said, "Ney, we are interested in your doing a book on the content of your messages."

Then Sharon Fischer, also in our publications department, commented to a mutual friend, "I've heard some of Ney's tapes. The things she is speaking on cross the lines of male, female, married, single . . . they apply to all of us. If she ever writes a book, I'd really like to work with her on it."

And so the Lord began to put it all together.

Feelings are a part of each of us. They can either be friend or foe depending on how we utilize them. Come with me now as I share with you some of the struggles and trials I've had in learning how to harness and channel my feelings. Come with me as I share how I've learned to use them as an avenue to take me to God's Word.

Hundreds of people who have heard the words on the following pages have come, called or written to say their lives will never be the same for having heard these truths. My desire is that each one who reads this book will be encouraged and challenged. I pray that God will "strike fire" in our hearts, that lives will be changed for the better and that everyone who finishes the book can say, "Now I understand how to walk by faith and how to take God at His word. Now I understand that faith is not a feeling, but a choice."

Ney Bailey
Lake Arrowhead, California

CONTENTS

The Flood

"Evacuate immediately! Evacuate immediately!" Those nightmarish words from the night before resounded in my head as I listened intently to the television newscast.

"July 31, 1976. The Big Thompson runs wild. Over its banks. One hundred people are dead, 800 missing; property damage in the millions; the worst disaster in Colorado state history. A freak rainstorm at the eastern face of the Continental Divide dumps 14 inches of rain in six hours from Estes Park to Loveland, just north of Denver. A wall of water hurdles down the canyon, pushed by a wailing, moaning wind. Trees are uprooted, homes and autos smashed to pieces. Rescue efforts bog down. Rescuers go airborne, searching desperately for the missing. The air itself a mixture of sewage, diesel fuel and human cries.

"By August first it is all over but the search .... The flood that experts thought impossible had hit, surging waters had turned a pastoral scene into a nightmare land-scape. There would be prayers of thanksgiving for the survivors; prayers of grief for those not as fortunate ...."

My thoughts drifted into the haunting retrospect of the TV announcer's voice. Just hours earlier I had been one of the flood's missing. I would soon learn that seven of the dearest people I knew were among the dead.

Our overnight retreat at the Sylvan Dale Ranch had been eagerly anticipated by the 35 of us in women's leadership positions with Campus Crusade for Christ. We wanted to be together for some "catch up" time before joining the annual Campus Crusade Staff Training at Colorado State University in Fort Collins.

It was like a family reunion. Our different ministries had spread us all over the United States the past year, and a few women were just returning from overseas assignments. We arrived at the ranch around noon on July 31, welcomed by a sign at its entrance, "Spend cool restful nights away from highway noise."

The weather was perfect. A bristling pine scent filled the mountain air. A warm sun eased its way through Rocky-Mountain clear blue skies onto our ranch which was nested in a valley at about 5,000 feet elevation. Through the Narrows, a sheer rock canyon towering next to the ranch, rushed the Big Thompson River.

After a relaxing lunch in the dining room overlooking the river, we went horseback riding and swimming. Climbing aboard a pile of hay on a wagon we sang and laughed and talked, as the wagon wound us up a narrow canyon road along the river to a waterfall and back to the ranch for the evening meal.

During the dinner hour, a silver-haired lady flyfishing in the river intrigued me as I gazed out a window. She was standing on some rocks in the river bed, her pants legs rolled up and her friends nearby encouraging her on. How, I wondered, could she hope to catch any fish in such fast-running water that was so shallow?

After our barbequed, home-cooked chicken dinner, our group gathered near a large stone fireplace in the spacious meeting room of the People's Barn, a quaint structure that faced the riverbank, decorated on the outside with large old wagon wheels.

The room was full of joy as many of us reflected aloud on all God had done for us through the year. Then I asked Carol Rhoad to tell her experience of that afternoon. Tired and in need of rest, she had gone to sleep and missed the hayride. After awakening she began visiting with one of the ranch owners.

"We have people here all the time, but I have never seen a group so happy, so peaceful, so beautiful," he had remarked. "Who are you?"

Carol took the occasion to explain to him the Source of our joy, and how he could know Jesus Christ as his Savior, too. Little did Carol know as she shared her afternoon experience with us that evening that in a matter of hours she would be with Jesus Christ—forever.

Marilyn Henderson explored with us her hopes and dreams for the upcoming Staff Training. She said she had prayed that "none of us would leave the same as when we came." We had no idea the next few hours and days would irrevocably change all our lives.

At about 9:15 we took a leisurely coffee break. We had been reassembled only a few minutes when I heard a siren ringing faintly in the distance. Within moments megaphone-muffled voices of the police joined the siren. As the noisy chorus approached, I began to distinguish the warning words. We were being told to evacuate—the river was rising, flood waters were coming.

"It's a joke," I thought.

Someone quickly offered, "I went outside at the coffee break, and the river did look a little funny . . . "

Everything seemed out of context. The day had been tranquil and sunny—except for what seemed, then, to be nonthreatening overcast and light sprinkling about dinner time.

Now the police were bellowing their orders in desperate repetition.

"Evacuate immediately! High water is coming! Don't take

anything with you . . . get to higher ground!"

The room was electric with action. In less than a minute we abandoned the People's Barn and dashed into the darkness, piling into eight cars.

We were all unfamiliar with our surroundings; no one really knew where to go. In the confusion we separated. Four cars stayed on the ranch, going in several different directions. The other four cars, including mine, followed the police across a bridge up to a store parking lot on Highway 34.

When I reached the parking lot, one of my passengers hopped out to seek directions while I kept the motor running. Just then someone standing nearby turned to announce, "The bridge we just crossed—it's gone!"

A policeman in a yellow rainslicker, illuminated only by car lights, was repeating through a megaphone the orders to higher ground. Above the incredible clamor of running car motors, people shouting and the exploding of propane tanks barreling down the river, I tried to scream, "*Where* is higher ground?"

There was no answer, only the policeman's continuous, frantic yell. "Can't you hear those tanks exploding? Get out of here . . . Get out of your cars and get to higher ground!"

I got out of my car and cried out again for some hint of direction. Again, no answer.

I knew that somewhere on the other side of the road the ground rose, but where? Eight of us from the parking lot group climbed out of our cars, and in the encircling darkness began groping our way up a steep hill in straggling formation.

The air was thick with the smell of propane gas. I could taste it in my mouth as we pulled ourselves up the mountain through the darkness and rain and confusion, fighting barbed wire, slipping in the mud.

Winky Leinster and I moved on hand-in-hand, aided only by lightning flashes that intermittently relieved the stormy blackness. We glanced back to see Jackie Hudson bending down to aid an elderly woman who was helplessly battling the wet mud, struggling to maneuver through the treacherous wire fence.

I had never felt so close to death. It seemed as if the raging water was nipping at our heels, following us up the mountain, threatening to swallow us any minute.

When we reached the top of the mountain, eight of us huddled together, not knowing where our friends were, nor understanding all that was happening around us. The mountain air was chilled, its cold intensified by biting winds and the pelting rain. I had always hated to be cold, but I refused to think about that now. As I sat on a rock just behind one of the women, I tried to shelter her from the pounding elements.

As we all faced each other in our closely-knit circle, I ventured, "Let's pray."

With a sense of authority of Scripture undergirding me I began, "Lord, Your Word says, 'In everything give thanks, because this is the will of God in Christ Jesus' concerning us.[1] So while we are in this, we choose with our wills to thank You.

"And Lord, Your Word says, 'All things'—including this— 'work together for good to those who love You'—and we do— 'and are called according to Your purpose'—and we are.[2] You have also said that heaven and earth will pass away before Your Word passes away.[3] So Your Word is truer than anything we are feeling or experiencing right now."

Our fears were calmed, our hearts comforted and strangely peaceful as we prayed together on that turbulent hilltop. Our prayers turned into song: *Father, we adore You. We lay our lives before You. How we love You* . . . After a time we descended the mountain a short distance to join a group of other tourists better sheltered by high rocks.

Snuggled against a large boulder was the older lady whom Jackie Hudson had helped through the fence. From our vantage point on the rocks we could still see propane tanks detonating in sudden, fiery bursts of light. And we could see the eerie flashing of headlights from vehicles being carried down the river.

Soon the police signaled us to come down. We were instructed to retrieve our cars, and before long we were following the highway patrol on a back road to Loveland.

Near Loveland, the flashing red lights of a police barricade flagged us on to Ft. Collins; they were not letting cars stop in Loveland.

We arrived in Ft. Collins after midnight. We then checked in with the sheriff's office about the safety of everyone else who had been at our retreat. They assured us that the Sylvan Dale Ranch had been evacuated safely. We wanted to go back and look for our friends, but a radio bulletin sounded: "Stay away from Loveland . . . to come would only add to the confusion and hamper rescue efforts!" Deciding there was nothing else we could do, we all went home.

Alone in my apartment next to the CSU campus, I pondered the evening's dizzying sequence of events. I was especially concerned that Marilyn Henderson had not yet arrived back at her apartment. Marilyn was my roommate during the year and a close friend and colleague. After leaving a note on her door, I went to bed. It was 3 a.m.

I awakened six hours later to the shocking, stunning news. I learned that it had been announced in the morning Staff Training meeting that some of our women were believed missing. Within minutes I had dressed, called my family to assure them of my safety and was racing to the office of Dr. Bill Bright, president of Campus Crusade.

People who were gathered near his door hugged me as I came up, grateful just to see me alive. For the first time since the warning sirens rang out along the river bank, almost 12 hours earlier, my tears began to flow.

Dr. Bright warmly welcomed me into his office. The atmosphere was solemn but peaceful.

"Ney, I'm so glad to see that you're safe. How did you get out?" he asked.

"The police led us out on a back road." I explained what happened to our group.

"Marilyn called about midnight to tell us she was in the

hospital," he said soberly. "Later they brought in Melanie (Ahlquist)."

I was bewildered. "What do you mean, they're in the hospital?"

"Their car went into the water. They don't think the others with them made it. Marilyn and Melanie were both hanging on to trees and were rescued."

"Their car went into the water?"

Dr. Bright continued calmly. "They were told to go east, toward Loveland."

"East toward Loveland!" I exclaimed.

I sat motionless, my mouth open in unbelief. Just then Dr. Bright was called to the phone. He listened intently and then placed his hand over the mouthpiece. He turned and looked at me.

"They've positively identified the bodies of Carol Rhoad and Cathie Loomis."

I slumped back in the chair as if I had been hit with a thousand-pound weight. The incredulity of the night before was seeping over into this Sunday morning.

After a few minutes more with Dr. Bright I hurried to the hospital and to Marilyn's room.

She smiled weakly when I entered. I remember when I saw her my thoughts formed the words of a song we had heard earlier in the summer, *That ain't no way to treat a lady* . . . We greeted one another warmly. She was bruised and exhausted, spitting up mud and debris from the violent river that had tried to claim her life.

The darkened sky looked almost as if the heart of God were mourning—rain was pouring down as I left the hospital late that afternoon to pick up Mary Graham, another close friend and co-worker, at the Denver Stapleton Airport. Mary had a prior commitment that had kept her from joining us at the retreat, and it had been pre-arranged that either Carol Rhoad or I would meet Mary as she stepped off the plane. I wanted Mary to know firsthand why Carol wasn't there.

I walked through the airport, practically in a daze. I had been in airports all over the country, hundreds of times, but this time was different. I reflected on all the people, passing back and forth to and from planes, having no idea that I had been in the flood the night before, that my heart was broken, that my friends were dead, injured or missing. No one knew the devastation I felt.

I wondered how many times I had passed people in airports who had just lost someone dear to them—and I had no way of knowing.

Over the next few days, the story began to piece together. Apparently, in the noise and confusion of the flood's onslaught, no one knew where to go to reach higher ground. Everyone was hearing different directions. Seventeen of our women managed to find each other on the ranch and spent the night in the Sylvan Dale recreation hall, hiking out to safety the next afternoon. Our meeting room in the People's Barn was filled to the ceiling with mud and water only minutes after we had evacuated.

Four cars made it across the bridge. Two carloads of us followed instructions to abandon our vehicles and climb on foot to higher ground.

The other cars obeyed a policeman's directions to travel east, toward Loveland. As they hit a low spot in the road, a wall of water crashed over the road, sweeping them into the river. Their cars sank within seconds.

Seven of the nine women in that group lost their lives. The two survivors, Marilyn and Melanie, fought for their lives, clinging to trees until rescuers reached them.

Throughout the following days, as we spent hours in the hospital caring for the needs of Marilyn and Melanie and carrying on the responsibilities of Staff Training, I remembered having read that whatever brings us the greatest joy also brings us the greatest sorrow. I knew that to be true as I cried over the death of my friends. I sobbed. I was broken-hearted. I had loved them dearly.

Vivid memories came back about each one.

Rae Ann Johnston . . . the morning of the retreat I slipped her a note during a meeting asking her to room with me . . . The note was tucked away in my Bible with her response, "I'd love to" . . .

Carol Rhoad . . . she had joyfully served as our secretary . . . she brought a touch of home to our regular meetings— surprises of fruit, cheese, flowers . . . Earlier in the summer I had given a four-week series of talks . . . Carol brought friends and was in the front row each time, cheering me on . . .

Cathie Loomis . . . Cathie was sitting by me in the People's Barn during the coffee break . . . I remember thinking, "I have never seen Cathie so radiantly beautiful" . . . There was a glow about her . . .

June Fujiwara . . . her eyes disappeared when she smiled her lovely Hawaiian smile . . . She stayed at my home in California one December—I snapped a picture of June on snow skiis for the first time in her life . . .

Precy Manongdo . . . our traveling representative in the Philippines . . . We had visited just that afternoon as we leaned over a fence, chatting and watching a stream go by, waiting for our horses to be saddled . . .

Barbie Leyden . . . she had been a delight to me ever since we met . . . Barbie had created a fictitious character named "Edith"—if the dishes didn't get done, it was Edith's negligence; if the car keys were missing, Edith was the culprit . . . One summer we planned a birthday party for Barbie's invisible friend, promising all the invited guests that she would actually appear . . . After refreshments we arranged for a telegram to be delivered—from Edith . . . The closing line? "You can't have your cake and Edith too" . . .

Terri Bissing . . . during a difficult two-week period in my life she sent me a card and special note every day in the mail . . . At the retreat we had planned to have a good visit . . .

Now they were gone. I would miss them terribly, and words couldn't express what was in my heart. I wanted to visit each family and tell them how special each woman was.

I also knew I was capable of becoming bitter and cynical if I dwelt on the loss and tragedy of it all, trying to answer the "whys" to which there were no real answers.

But I had learned from previous experience that we become bitter to the degree that we don't give thanks to God, so through my tears I began to offer a "sacrifice of thanksgiving."[4] I made my heart attitude one of gratefulness to God. I purposed to focus on what He had given rather than on what was gone.

I realized I could have lived my life without ever knowing and loving these dear women, yet God had allowed me to enjoy them. He had given me the gift of time spent with each person.

I had to choose with my will, not my feelings, to give thanks over and over again. God, in His Word, had promised that He would work *all things* (including this tragedy) together for good to those who love Him and are called according to His purpose.

A month or so after the flood, a friend wrote from Europe, "Ney, if I had been in that flood, I don't know if I could have had your response."

I was deeply aware that this was not a natural response for me, but a supernatural one—of believing God's Word was truer than how I felt. I was also deeply aware that it was a result of many years in which I had learned lessons the hard way—by my mistakes.

2

Arizona Agony

My navy-blue Volkswagen "bug" was packed to the gills. I had stuffed most of my earthly belongings into my little car and a four-by-eight trailer hitched behind it. Ahead lay the desolate, 1,700-mile journey from home in New Orleans, across west Texas, New Mexico and into Arizona, a trip that would eventually find me in Tucson—to begin my first year of ministry with Campus Crusade at the University of Arizona.

There was much to think about in those lonely hours on the road. I was embarking on a new adventure. At 25 my life had been filled with many successes, great joys and few disappointments. And although Jesus Christ became my Savior when I was 15, it was not until I had graduated from college and was working in New Orleans as an adoption caseworker that I gave my life to Christ. Thus my sense of real commitment to Him was only about a year and a half old. Young, confident and hopeful, I enthusiastically anticipated doing "great things" for God.

At our staff conference a month before I had been interviewed by one of the conference leaders.

"What do you think is your greatest need as you look forward to your assignment?" he had asked.

Without hesitation I said, "To be trained in a campus ministry, because I've never seen one." Having been impressed with the caliber of men and women at the conference, I wanted to grow in my faith, to be able to do what they did, to know what they knew.

Now the road signs indicated that my trip was nearly over. I had heard much about this desert country, its year-round sun, the exquisite sunsets. Hundreds of large Saguaro cacti decorated the valleys in multitudes of shapes framed by hills and mountains in the distance. I loved Arizona already.

A thoughtful couple had found a one-room apartment for me adjacent to one of the university's largest dormitories. At the time all I really knew of the school was that the previous year it was voted No. 1 "party" school in the nation by *Playboy* magazine. But driving into Tucson and past the university toward my apartment, a beautiful campus emerged, with tall palm trees and white buildings with red tile roofs.

I arrived on the scene with great expectations, anxious to jump into my training, eager to learn everything there was to know. A staff man, Paul Schipper, had been assigned to work on the campus with me. I also was eager to get to know the student who had initiated the ministry on campus, whom I had heard possessed a wealth of information and "know-how."

But suddenly the tables turned. Our student leader, needing to free himself of extra responsibilities, turned the entire ministry over to Paul and me in order to devote his full attention to graduate studies. And within days after our arrival, Paul was sent 120 miles north to Arizona State University for training by the area's staff director, Elmer Lappen.

Much to my chagrin, I was left at the University of Arizona, in unfamiliar Tucson—ALONE.

Evidently my background had been considered, and it was assumed that I could handle the responsibility. Now, having barely arrived, the entire operation was mine to run. This was not what I'd had in mind at all.

I was usually ready to try anything. I remember thinking on the drive out to Arizona, "I've been a 'student leader,' Lord, so when I get to campus I'll talk to all the student leaders about You. I've been a dorm president, so I'll talk to them. I've been a sorority officer, so I'll go talk to all the sorority officers. I was a class officer, so I'll make appointments to see the class officers."

But now that I had arrived, my past credentials certainly weren't supplying me with any confidence. Where was the old boldness and enthusiasm? Before I left Louisiana a number of people had become Christians through my sharing the gospel with them. I had been eager to reach out to others. But here in Arizona I had to make myself head for campus each day. In fact, I was quite relieved when an appointment with a student didn't materialize—it left me with lots of time for browsing in the nearby bookstore or the chance to employ other proven methods of procrastination until lunchtime or dinner.

I was also feeling certain pressures of performance. Some of these were imposed externally; Campus Crusade had set up some guidelines and standards for every staff member. While desperately wanting to live up to those standards, I felt I couldn't. And I usually didn't.

Other pressures were self-imposed. Without knowing exactly how to do my job, I still expected that I should do it as well as I had done anything else. Not only that, but I compared myself to other staff members and, in my mind anyway, came up quite short.

Diane Ross, for example, was my ideal. Diane (now Diane Hutcheson) was our women's national traveling representative at that time, highly successful in her ministry and seemingly always on top of things. It was obvious that Diane knew the Word of God, and she seemed to share her faith in Christ freely and easily with others. She was a lovely person in every way. On my personal scale of comparison, Diane rose to the top—and I landed on the bottom.

But perhaps more earthshaking than my fears or feelings of inadequacy was my disillusionment with God. I felt like He had let me down.

After all, hadn't I left behind in Louisiana my family, my friends, my security? Hadn't I "left all" to follow Jesus Christ? Now it seemed as if the rug were being pulled out from under my life. Is this what it meant to serve Him?

I wondered how I had ever gotten myself in such a predicament. Even more, I wondered how I would ever get out of it. My first month in Arizona was barely gone, and I wanted to quit.

Never before in my life had I been a failure—at least to admit it to others. Oh, failure experiences came to mind, but there were "reasons" for them. Once I had failed a high school algebra course but "only because the teacher was so hard." I soon took it over with another teacher and passed.

I recalled another incident from college days. Our school choir was a prestigious musical organization, held in high regard all over the state of Louisiana. I auditioned for the choir and for some unknown reason was accepted, possibly because I could hit some low notes and the choir needed altos. During pre-season practice at choir camp I stayed close to the other altos, able to depend on them for pitch and cues.

As was his custom, the director soon separated all the different singing parts so that altos, sopranos, tenors and basses were mixed together. And suddenly there were no longer any altos to lean on. Since I couldn't read the music or sound it out "by ear," I began mouthing the words in rehearsal, making certain never to sing loudly enough for anyone to hear me unless I was absolutely sure of my note.

But real panic set in when the choir's performing plans for the year were announced. Aside from the normal round of traveling concerts, we were scheduled on a weekly television program and would possibly be selected by the government for a tour of Asian military bases.

That was when I made my decision: I just couldn't stay in the choir and fake it, not with that kind of itinerary. Something had to be done.

Yet, rather than admit my failure right then, I began to stew over my dilemma. Finally, after mulling over every possible means of face-saving retreat from the choir, a solution came to me: one thing that would guarantee my dismissal.

One day I was alone in my sorority house. Taking out a three-foot high stool, I placed it in the middle of the living room. Then I began jumping off the stool, over and over—in desperate hopes that my ankle would break, thereby disabling me from standing up for any performances. Years before my ankle was hurt on a hiking trip, and I thought surely it would "re-injure" this time.

I ended up with a very sore foot—and enough of an excuse to be released from further rehearsal with the choir. I did feel a tinge of sadness when the choir went to Asia without me, but I also knew that no one had knocked me out of going along— but me.

And now, too, I didn't want to admit failure. What would people think? How could I write Bill Bright and tell him I hated Arizona already? There were people back home praying for me and investing financially in my ministry. How could I possibly write them and say I wasn't going through with my assignment?

Late one afternoon I was lying down on the rug in my little apartment, my head resting on my arms. As I lay there I could see lines on the wall marking where my bed opened out of the wall. Then my eyes spotted the gas heater on the next wall.

"I'll just turn on that gas heater, and it will all be over. All my misery will be gone."

I thought again. "No, that would never do, because immediately the Tucson newspaper headlines would read, 'Campus Crusade staff member commits suicide!' And that would reflect negatively on Campus Crusade, on Christ, on me!"

My imagination drifted to the mountain range near Tucson. "I'll go up to Mt. Lemon in my little Volkswagen, and just happen to be driving down the mountain, and I'll go off the side . . . it'll look like an accident! And everyone will say, 'Poor Ney, she was out for a leisurely drive on the mountain and somehow lost control of the car . . . '"

There! No negative reflection on me, on Campus Crusade, or on the Lord. That seemed to be an honorable way out.

Despite this fleeting contemplation of "ending it all," I spent most of my time thinking, "Lord, if I can ever get out of this place, I'll never come back."

When the first of November came and I was scheduled to travel up to Arizona State University for training, I jumped at the chance. "If I can only get up there," I told myself, "everything will be all right." But I soon discovered that a change in location wasn't the solution to my problems. If you take a rotten apple and fly it from Tucson to Phoenix, it's still rotten when it gets there. And I took my "rotten apple" with me. I hated Arizona State too—finding myself still depressed, still afraid and still feeling like a failure.

One day, when I was scheduled to be on campus, I defiantly jumped in my Volkswagen, drove to Phoenix and found a coffee shop. I ordered the biggest hot fudge sundae on the menu.

"Here I am, eating this hot fudge sundae," I proclaimed with belligerence. "Nobody knows I'm here, I don't need this, and I DON'T CARE!"

I had been invited to be in the wedding of a childhood friend named Bev, in Corpus Christi, Texas, around Christmas time. I mentioned the wedding to Elmer Lappen when we met for our weekly appointment in the library.

"Elmer, when I go home for Christmas to be in Bev's wedding, I think I'll stay there and not come back."

He looked at me sadly. "Ney, if you do that, it will break my heart."

And I thought firmly, "I care more about getting out of here than I do about breaking Elmer's heart."

But at long last December 15 arrived, the day of my departure for Bev's wedding and Christmas vacation. I had never been so glad to leave a place in my entire life. I jumped in my VW, hit the city limits of Tucson, stopped, bought a package of Kents and a package of Salems and smoked all the way to Corpus Christi!

I had smoked rarely throughout my life, and when I did it was usually symptomatic of something that was wrong in my life. By the time I arrived at Bev's wedding rehearsal I smelled like a tobacco factory.

At the rehearsal dinner, someone suggested we each mention briefly what Bev meant to us. I loved her dearly—but that night I was tongue-tied. Bev had been my primary influence for joining Campus Crusade staff. I was miserable and reasoned that she had contributed to my state of mind. I didn't say a word, and felt even worse!

I headed for my family home in Shreveport, Louisiana, following the wedding. I barely enjoyed Christmas and moped around the house for two weeks. One day, as the end of my vacation approached, I found myself sitting on our living room couch, gazing toward the dining room and occasionally out the living room's large picture window. I was feeling sorry for myself and dreading the thought of returning to Arizona.

Holding up my hand I began to count on my fingers. "September, October, November, December . . . let's see, I've made it through four months." I continued counting. "January, February, March, April, May . . . I guess if I've made it through four months, I can make it through five more. But in May—I'm quitting."

Driving back to Arizona was one of the hardest things I've ever done. But awaiting me at my apartment was a letter from a friend in Hawaii. He wrote, "Ney, I recently heard a man speak who helped me tremendously. His name is Merv Rosell, and for me, he was God's man with God's message at just the right time. He's going to be in Phoenix, and I want you to hear him."

I thought, "If there's ever anything I've needed, it's God's man with God's message—and this has got to be the right time."

Within a week I was on my way to hear Merv Rosell. I remember thinking in the car, "Missionary or not, Lord, if I have to, I'll even walk down an aisle tonight to get right with You. I'm willing to do whatever You want me to do."

I arrived at the meeting, not believing my ears as I heard the subject of his evening message: "Defeated Christians."

Rosell began, "If you have ever felt defeated in your Christian walk, this message is for you." I listened as if I were the only person in the room. He spoke of trying to live the Christian life on one's own resources, through self-effort. And he remarked that God often allows failure—to point us to one crucial truth: that we cannot live the Christian life on our own.

In conclusion, he said, "If you want to live for Jesus Christ this year, and the rest of your life, and if you want Jesus Christ to begin to live through you, I want you to stand."

I had been in other meetings where "invitations" were given. Usually I looked around self-consciously just to see if anyone else was going to respond.

But this night I didn't care. It now had dawned on me that I was trying to live the Christian life myself—depending on my own efforts. I desperately wanted Christ to begin living His life through me. I rose to my feet, and in that moment surrendered my will, and my whole being, into the control of the Lord Jesus Christ. The Lord's presence became as real to me as when I first trusted Him as Savior.

For such a long time God had seemed so distant. I couldn't bear the thought that even though He seemed so much closer right now He might go away again. I left the meeting thinking, "Lord, I've been aware of Your presence for 10 minutes. Please don't go away!"

I drove home, and when I stepped out of the car I prayed, "Lord, for 30 minutes now we've had unbroken fellowship. Please don't go away!" Just before falling asleep, I knelt beside my bed. "Please be here in the morning, Lord, when I wake up."

The next morning He was there. And we made it through the day together. And the next day. And the next. A whole week. The month.

It seemed like I had been all alone through those first months in Tucson. But He who had promised to stay with me always, had been with me—even when I didn't recognize His presence. God wasn't surprised that I had been in the "wilderness." It was He who had led me there.

Though I had gone to Arizona with the purest of intentions, following the Lord the best I knew how, I now understood I had gone in my own power, on the strength of my own merits, with my own desires and expectations. And God had allowed me to fail miserably, so much that I wanted to die. He let me hit the depths.

But out of those depths of frustration, I called upon Him. And He answered, revealing to me that there was only one person who had lived perfectly the Christian life—Jesus Christ Himself. When I began asking Christ to live His life through me, in the power of His Spirit, He began to do through me what I could not do for myself.

If anything of eternal value was going to be accomplished through me, Christ would have to do it.

I think it is possible that when we present ourselves to God for service, He may look at us with our pride and self-sufficiency and say,

> *I love you, but I need to tear down what is not of My Spirit, so I can build back up.*
> *I need to wound you so I can heal you.*
> *I see you depending upon your own strength.*
> *I see you depending upon yourself.*
> *I need to let you experience failure—so you will call on Me and depend upon Me for your life and strength.*

I thought, of course, that Campus Crusade had made a terrible mistake to put me in Tucson all alone. Yet I know, now, that the Lord placed me there. My "fiery furnace" of Arizona was God's special way of performing His refining work in my character—His way of beginning to teach me to walk by faith. But He didn't stop there.

3

Just Say the Word

Pouring myself a glass of ice-cold lemonade, I pulled out my legal pad, sharpened a pencil and eagerly began to work on my research. Earlier in the day the professor of my summer school Bible course had given me an assignment.

"Bring back to the class a report on everything the book of Romans has to say about faith," he had instructed. That sounded very exciting and fairly easy.

I was in for a surprise.

As I moved through the chapters of Romans, the word "faith" appeared almost too many times to count. As I pondered the word, I found myself asking, "What is it? Faith is probably the most important thing in my life, but how do I define it?"

My mind flashed back eight years to my time in Tucson when I had not understood a walk of faith. "I've come so far in my understanding," I thought. And yet I felt puzzled as I asked myself again, "What *is* faith?"

I knew that throughout the Bible there were hundreds of references to faith, such as "The just shall live by faith"[1] and "This is the victory that has overcome the world—our faith."[2] I was astonished that I couldn't come up with a simple, personalized definition of the word; I had never completed the statement: "For me, faith is _____ ."

I thought, "Lord, how would You define it?"

A story came to mind in which Jesus had said to someone,

"Not even in Israel have I found such great faith." I became quite curious. What was it that Jesus Himself called "great faith?"

I quickly looked up the passage in Luke 7.

There I found the story of a centurion who was willing to believe that Jesus could heal a loyal and trusted servant who was near death. He said to Jesus, " . . . Just say the word, and my servant will be healed."[3] Then the centurion used a personal example to illustrate that he understood what it meant to be taken at his word.

Jesus' response to the centurion was to turn to the crowd that was following Him and say, "I say to you, not even in Israel have I found such great faith."[4] So it seemed to me that Jesus was calling "great faith" simply taking Him at His word.

I wondered if such a "definition" would be confirmed elsewhere in Scripture. Since Hebrews 11 is often referred to as "faith's hall of fame," I turned there.

After reading and re-reading the passage with all its references to the phrase "By faith . . . , " I began to see a common denominator throughout the chapter's examples. No matter whom the writer of Hebrews was talking about, each person had simply taken God at His word and obeyed His command. And they were remembered for their faith.

For example, God told Noah to build an ark.

Noah took God at His word and built the ark. Therefore, Hebrews 11:7 begins, "By faith Noah . . . " Throughout the chapter, it appeared that regardless of the circumstances, despite arguments of logic and reason—even regardless of how he *felt*, each person mentioned believed God and His word and chose to be obedient.

By now, my homework had become far more exciting than I could have imagined. I began to wonder, "If Luke 7 and Hebrews 11 illustrate great faith, what about an illustration of a lack of faith?"

I remembered an incident from Mark 4 where Jesus had

lack of faith Fdd

just finished a full day of preaching and teaching by the shores of Galilee. He instructed the disciples to go to the other side of the sea. They took Jesus at His word initially, got into a boat with Him and headed for the other side. But when a storm arose, they lost confidence in Christ's words that they would actually reach the other shore. When Jesus asked them, "How is it that you have no faith?"[5] He could just as easily have said, "How is it that you are not taking Me at My word?"

His word proved to be true. I have always loved the first verse of Mark 5, "And they came to the other side of the sea."

On the basis of all I observed in these passages, I had arrived at a simple, workable definition of faith! I wasn't sure if I would ever have a report on all the book of Romans said about faith, but in my own heart I knew I had learned something that would prove to be very significant in my walk with God.

But I had one more question. If faith is a matter of taking God at His word, what does God say about His word? I found the answer in Scripture itself.

"Heaven and earth will pass away, but My Words shall not pass away."[6]

" . . . The word of the Lord abides forever."[7]

"The grass withers, the flower fades, but the word of our God stands forever."[8]

These verses were telling me that everything in life may change, but God's Word remains constant! His truth never changes. I was beginning to catch a glimpse of how this could affect me the rest of my life.

For instance, I am the kind of person who feels things very deeply. There are times when I am so happy I think I will never be sad again. Then there are other times when I am so sad I think I will never be happy again.

But as strong as my feelings are, it was encouraging for me to realize that

> God's Word is truer than anything I feel.
> God's Word is truer than anything I experience.
> God's Word is truer than any circumstance I will ever face.
> God's Word is truer than anything in the world.

Why?

Because heaven and earth will pass away before God's Word will pass away. This meant that no matter how I felt or what I experienced, I could choose dependence on the Word of God as the unchanging reality of my life.

I look back on that summer evening and that "simple" research project as a turning point in my life. Innumerable times since then, when circumstances and feelings have seemed more real than life itself, I've chosen to believe that God's Word is truer than anything else. I've chosen, as it were, to walk by faith. Sometimes that choice has been a difficult one to make.

For example, there were times after that when I could say, "I don't feel loved." I could choose to dwell on that feeling, letting it carry me on into a state of self-pity, or I could say, "Lord, I don't feel loved. That is the truth. That is where I am right now.

"But, Lord, Your Word says that You love me. In fact, You've said that You have loved me with an everlasting love.[9] You never stop loving me. Your love for me is the one thing that stands when all else has fallen. Your Word says there is no partiality with You.[10] That means You don't love anyone else in the world more than You love me. So, Lord, I thank You now that I'm loved. And I'll keep on going, knowing that I am loved by You. Your Word is truer than how I feel."

I began to realize that the important thing about this kind of response is that it gave me the freedom to be honest with the Lord and freedom to acknowledge my feelings, while at the same time believing God's Word.

There have been other times when I have felt afraid or lonely or depressed. During some of these periods my heart has literally ached in anguish over the circumstances of life, and in those moments I have been the most tempted to doubt the truth of God's Word. But they were the points at which I had to *choose with my will* to believe His Word. Thousands of times my prayers have begun,

"Lord, I *feel* . . . but, Lord, *Your Word* says . . . " ✗

And I've found that He does bring my emotions in line with ✗ His Word, in His own timing and in His way.

The Bible promises that, for those of us who truly love God, everything that happens in our lives will have the effect of molding us into Christ's image.[11] Some of us may have prayed a prayer similar to this, "Lord, I pray You'd make me more like You. I pray that You would conform me to the image of Christ." Often what we want is for the Lord to give us an "anesthetic" so that one day we'll suddenly wake up totally conformed to Christ's perfect character.

But He doesn't work that way. He allows the trials, temptations and pressures of life to come so that we have the opportunity to respond either by the way we feel or by taking Him at His Word.

The Lord is concerned about what we go through, but I believe He is more concerned with how we respond to what we go through. That response is a matter of our wills.

I have learned to get into the habit of taking God at His Word—and it is a habit! We can either grow accustomed to listening to our feelings, thoughts and circumstances, letting them control us, or we can be in the habit of taking God at His Word. We need to choose with our wills to believe that His Word is truer than our feelings.

I have made a lifetime commitment to bank my life on the Word of God—and God has honored that commitment.

And yet, there have been times since I made that decision when it would have been much easier to go back on it, because I couldn't believe that anything was truer than what I was going through; times when my feelings have screamed 180 degrees in the opposite direction of God's Word.

In fact, there have been lots of times . . .

4

Matters of Conscience

One bright August morning in 1969, I was dressing for work, my television set tuned to NBC's Today Show. I hadn't been listening closely to the program, but suddenly a newscaster's voice caught my attention.

"Yesterday, Arab and Israeli jets engaged in confrontation over the Sinai desert," he announced.

In his very next breath, the newscaster remarked, "Evangelist Billy Graham stated last night that he believes Jesus Christ is coming again soon."

I was stunned. To me, it seemed incredible to hear those two events announced one right after the other over national television. The NBC reporter hadn't connected the two incidents, but I had.

Into my mind flashed Christ's words in Matthew 24, concerning the last days before His second coming. He promised wars, rumors of wars, famines and earthquakes, and false prophets setting out to mislead many. Then He said, "And because lawlessness is increased, most people's love will grow cold."[1]

I stood there in the middle of the room and prayed, "Lord, don't let my love toward You grow cold! Bring revival to our land, our world."

I remembered an old camp slogan, "All fires are the same size at the start." I continued, "You've got to begin somewhere, Lord. So begin with me. Bring revival to my heart."

That same week those desires and prayers were to be tested.

I was listening to a guest speaker during the summer's Staff Training at Arrowhead Springs, California, the international headquarters for Campus Crusade. The speaker had chosen as his topic the importance of maintaining a clear conscience.

We need to live in such a way, he said, that neither God nor man could point the finger at us and charge, "You've offended me, and you've never tried to make it right." He quoted the apostle Paul's declaration, "I also do my best to maintain always a blameless conscience both before God and before men."[2]

And, he continued, Paul warns Timothy in his first letter to the young disciple, " . . . Fight the good fight, keeping faith and a good conscience, which some have rejected and suffered shipwreck in regard to their faith."[3]

Our guest speaker urged us not to become introspective in the examining of our consciences. If, however, something needed to be made right in our relationships with God and man, it would surface effortlessly in our minds.

Up until this particular message, I had never given the subject much thought. But, immediately, three incidents clearly and unmistakably came to mind.

I gulped.

"No, Lord. Not that! Or that . . . or that! You don't mean I have to take care of *those*!?"

Then I heard the promptings of an inner voice. "Ney, did you mean it when you said you wanted the revival to begin with you?"

"Yes."

"Do you care more about your reputation with people or with Me?"

"I care more about my reputation with You."

"Ney, are you willing to make things right?"

"Yes, Lord, I'm willing."

The first experience I recalled had to do with my car insurance. In 1963 I had moved from Tucson to Arrowhead Springs to develop Campus Crusade's personnel department. I had been living on the headquarters grounds and received all my mail there.

Each time my car insurance was due, I would receive a notice to send the payment and a memo to sign which stated that the insurance company's information about me was accurate. The last line before the signature space read, "I do not drive more than 40 miles weekly to work." The statement was true of me—until I moved up into the mountains about 20 miles above Arrowhead Springs. The drive to and from work began averaging almost 200 miles a week.

After my move the notice once again came to my office at Arrowhead Springs. I was ready to sign the memo verifying all the information as correct, when I came to the mileage statement. I read it once again: "I do not drive more than 40 miles weekly to work."

The wheels of rationalization started clicking in my mind.

"I still get my mail here at Arrowhead Springs," I told myself. "Besides, the insurance company doesn't know I've moved, and my premium would probably go up if I told them . . . I think I'll just sign the memo and send it back."

Six months later another bill came, along with the memo. I signed it again.

Now, after hearing this talk, I knew my time had come. My stomach felt queasy and weak at the very thought of going to the local agent confessing my actions. But within a day or so I was on my way.

I had never done anything like this before. My hands were clammy as I parked my car in front of the agent's office, a refurbished home built in the 1920's. Slowly, deliberately, I went inside.

There were people in the waiting area as I walked through the door. My agent, Mr. Blevins, looked up, and with a friendly smile said, "May I help you?" My heart sank. I didn't want to tell the whole world my story.

"That's okay," I spoke hesitantly. "I don't mind waiting. I'd like to talk with you alone."

When everyone else had gone, he signaled me to follow him into his private office.

I sat down and swallowed hard, perspiration on my brow.

"Now, what can I do to help you?" the agent asked.

"Mr. Blevins, this may be one of the most unusual visits you've ever had." I explained to him what I had done, that I realized I had been wrong, and that I had come to make things right, paying back what I owed.

He listened intently as I spoke. As I concluded, his eyes misted with tears.

"Thank you for telling me that, Ney," he said. "Actually, we figure some people overpay, and some people underpay, so consider the matter settled."

I couldn't believe what he was saying.

"Are you sure?" I asked. "I'd really be glad to pay whatever I owe."

"No," he replied. "There's really no problem. You don't need to do anything. But I do appreciate your coming. By the way, you work up there with Campus Crusade, don't you?"

"Yes, I do."

He said warmly, "How's Ken Berven? I haven't see him lately."

"He's fine." For several minutes more we talked of the Lord and our mutual faith in Christ. Then I excused myself, thanking him for his time and understanding.

A flood of emotion overwhelmed me as I stepped out into the afternoon's sunshine; feelings of joy and relief and a sense of deep inner satisfaction. I had gone to make peace, to right a wrong. I had no earthly idea of how "right" God would make things. "Oh, Lord, thank You," I prayed. "Thank You, thank You for going before me and preparing the way."

The next incident I had to deal with concerned a loan I had

negotiated recently at the bank. I wanted to buy some stock that was just going on the market. A friend's father was starting a new company that was certain to be a smashing success, and I felt privileged to get in on the ground floor of the new venture.

It would be a perfect chance to build up a "nest egg" for the future, I thought. I dreamed of all the things I could buy for myself and for others as the stock skyrocketed in value. This was sure to be the deal of the century!

However, since I had no money to invest in the stock, I decided to borrow $1,000 from my bank. Since my car was nearly paid for, I knew it could be used as equity for the loan.

But when I filled out the forms at the bank, I didn't mention the fact that I would be using the money for investment in stock. I seemed to recall hearing that banks frowned upon loans taken out for something speculative such as stock. So, instead, I listed as the reasons for my request, "Clothes, vacation and miscellaneous."

As soon as the loan was approved, I rushed downtown to a well-known brokerage firm to purchase my stock. They had no listing for it. A broker I met there begged me not to buy, and he began offering me alternatives.

But I was determined to buy the stock. I had seen the prospectus and soon the whole world would know of this progressive new organization. I phoned a broker in the city where the company was located, who sold me the stock at $1.75 a share. Soon it had climbed to $2.50, then $3.00, on up to $4.00 a share. I was elated.

Within a week and a half I received notice from my company that it had come under investigation by the Securities and Exchange Commission. The commission was ordering the stock to be taken off the market immediately. The notice assured me, however, that this was only a temporary condition, and the company would quickly bounce back into competition. It has never recovered.

Not only did I begin paying back a loan which became a total financial loss for me, but I also learned that it was indeed illegal to borrow money for the purchase of stock.

Now, once again, I had to right a wrong.

I paid a visit to my loan officer at the bank and explained my story. Even though more than six months had passed since my investment fell through, she was, like Mr. Blevins my insurance agent, amazingly sympathetic and understanding. She said she realized I had probably learned a valuable, and expensive, lesson—and refused to press any penalties.

And when she learned I would soon be moving to Dallas, Texas, she gave me her professional card, suggesting that it might be helpful to use when I opened a new bank account there. She offered to help me in any way possible, even to serve as a reference in future financial transactions!

I left her office exultant and grateful to the Lord for what He had done.

It wasn't until later that I came across these verses in Proverbs: " . . . Hasty speculation brings poverty. Dishonest gain will never last."[4]

The third "confession" I had to make was probably the most difficult one of all for me.

In 1962, Campus Crusade initiated an Institute of Biblical Studies in order to give the staff in depth Bible training. That year, one of my courses was in the Gospel of John. For the course's final exam, we were given a closed-book, take-home quiz—to be completed on our honor.

I can clearly remember the afternoon I took the test. I was sitting on a top bunk in my small dorm room going over the questions. I came to a question which certainly sounded simple enough, but my mind completely blocked on the answer. I was sure I knew the answer, but at that moment I couldn't think of it to save my life.

I began reasoning, "All I need is one clue, just to get my mind working again." After I had completed all the other questions, I returned to the problem question. My mind was still blocked on the answer.

Then the inward struggle began. Should I . . . or shouldn't I? Back and forth I went. I finally gave in. I opened my Bible and closed it just as quickly. But it was enough to give me the clue I needed for the answer to the question.

I hadn't *really* cheated, I thought as I handed in the exam. I knew that answer and needed only a little help for its recall. But a heaviness slowly began to overtake me that day, and for days following. I confessed my sin to the Lord over and over, but my guilt didn't go away. It became difficult even to look at the Gospel of John, much less at the page from which I had sneaked a look.

With the passing of time, my guilt feelings subsided . . . except for occasions every once in awhile when something would remind me. Now, seven years later I was reminded, and my guilt surfaced again, loud and clear as a clanging bell.

This time I knew my reputation with people was really on the line. It was bad enough to cheat on any test. But a Bible test? It was distasteful to even think about! Again I was faced with the question: Do I care more about my reputation with people, or my reputation with the Lord? Was I "willing to be willing" to do the right thing?

I knew this confession could be harder than the other two. I didn't know if I would ever see the insurance agent or the bank officer again. But to admit my cheating to my professor, a fellow staff member . . .

That summer of 1969 the annual all-staff picnic was held in a lovely park in nearby Riverside, California. It was a beautiful day, and there was a festive atmosphere in the air when I arrived. But I didn't have the enthusiasm to enter into the games going on all around. I was thinking about the test.

I told myself that if Ted Martin, the director of IBS, came by I would tell him the whole story. But I was soon headed toward the opposite side of the park away from everyone else, and finding a secluded spot by a stream, I sat down at a redwood picnic table. I stared for long minutes at the table, then at the trees.

Presently I heard footsteps on an old curved wooden bridge about 20 feet behind me. I wheeled around. Was this a mirage? Or was it real? Dr. Martin, his wife, Gwen, and their four children were crossing the bridge and heading toward me. It wasn't a mirage.

The family came up to the table and greeted me. "Hey, Ney!" Dr. Martin smiled. "Whatcha doing 'way over here?"

"Oh, just thinking. Are you on your way to the picnic?"

Dr. Martin replied, "Yes, we were just out exploring, and now we're on our way back."

The family started to leave, but I knew this was the time to settle my account.

"Ted," I spoke hesitantly. "Could I talk to you a few minutes before you go?"

"Sure," he said, and the rest of his family kept walking toward the picnic.

With a quivering voice I began, "Ted, something happened seven years ago that I need to tell you about." I related the incident and finished by telling him I knew I had been wrong and that I was willing to talk to the professor of the course to make things right.

"No," Dr. Martin answered in an understanding voice. "Talking to me is good enough."

He went on, "Ney, we know that things like this go on from time to time. But you're the first person who has ever admitted anything. However, I think you've suffered enough. You don't need to do anything about it."

I gratefully acknowledged his kindness, and as he walked away I felt as though I could have joined the birds in the trees with little effort. Such a weight had been lifted that I practically skipped over to join the picnic, with praise and thanksgiving on my lips.

As I look back it seems as if I was unusually fortunate that each person so warmly received my admission of guilt. However,

I had no way of knowing that my insurance agent wouldn't say, "You owe me several hundred dollars plus penalties and interest." Or that the loan officer wouldn't reply, "For this, I'm afraid we'll have to press charges and take you to court. It will no doubt mean a sizable fine and possible jail sentence."

How did I know that Dr. Martin wouldn't say, "I'm afraid you're going to have to retake the course"? But regardless of their responses to me, I had to take the initiative to make things right.

And it wasn't the *measure* of wrong that determined whether or not I should deal with my different circumstances. The situations I encountered may or may not seem minor to others— obviously if I had robbed a bank, shoplifted or aimed a pistol at someone I would eventually have to face up to my actions. The fact that I committed wrongdoing, however minor, was enough to warrant efforts toward reconciliation.

Revival had begun in me. My conscience was clear in every relationship I could think of . . . or was it?

There was one I had forgotten.

5

A Change of Heart

Yesterday the phone rang. It was my mother calling.

"Honey, your daddy and I were talking this week, and he told me how proud he is of each of you children. 'I can't tell them myself,' he said, 'but I'd like for you to call each one of them and tell them for me how proud I am of them.'"

This was the call of a lifetime.

"Mother, he really said that?"

"Yes, he did."

"Will you say it for me the way he said it? Don't leave out a word."

"Your daddy wanted me to call and tell you how proud he is of you."

"Mother, will you say it just one more time?"

"Your daddy wanted me to call and tell you he is proud of you."

"Would you please tell him 'thank you' for me and that this is the best present I've ever received in all my life?"

I was elated as I hung up the phone. It was a momentous occasion for me. Because things haven't always been this way.

I remember when I was six years old.

I was barely three feet tall, standing on the edge of the municipal pool. "Jump, Ney Ann!" coaxed my father, his arms outstretched. "I'll catch you!"

The water was over my head where he was standing in the

pool. I was petrified to jump in.

I called out, trembling, "No, I can't do it!"

"Yes, you can," he shouted. "Jump, and I'll catch you!"

Finally I jumped. But my father wasn't there. My head went under the water, and I came up sputtering and thrashing. Daddy had moved back in the water, hoping I would swim to him. I began to cry.

"Daddy, you moved! You said you wouldn't!"

I heard him laughing. "Ney Ann, you've gotten upset over nothing. You know I wouldn't let anything happen to you. I was just trying to teach you to swim."

That experience had a devastating effect on my child-like mind. I had trusted Daddy with everything that my little heart could muster—Daddy had said he would catch me, but he didn't. He had let me down.

The experience was representative of how I began to feel about him as I grew older. I began to realize that some of the deepest hurts we'll ever know come from those we care most about, hurts which often result in bruised relationships within our families. And those relationships are often the hardest to heal. With many other experiences to fuel my feelings and attitudes, my bitterness toward my father was deeply-rooted —and full-grown—by the time I entered college.

It wasn't until after I left Arizona and moved to California to begin Campus Crusade's personnel department that I came to a turning point I wasn't even aware I needed.

I attended a meeting where one of our staff said some things I had never heard before. I knew that the Bible states, "God is love."[1] I also knew that I Corinthians 13 reveals what love is. But the speaker said one thing that was like bright sunshine piercing into a long-closed dungeon: "If God is love, and I Corinthians 13 tells what love is, then God loves you and God loves me with that same kind of love."

This was totally new to me.

I had always heard that I was supposed to love other people with a I Corinthians-13-kind-of-love. It had even been suggested that I test my own love for others by putting my name in where the chapter mentions "love." I failed the test! But it hadn't occurred to me to put God's name in the place of "love."

Now, I was discovering that God's love toward me is kind,
God's love toward me is patient,
God's love toward me is not
  provoked,
God's love toward me does not
  take into account a
  wrong suffered,
God's love toward me would
  bear all things,
  believe all things,
  hope all things,
  endure all things.
God's love toward me would
  never fail.

It was overwhelming to think He loved me in that way.

As I drove home from the meeting, I began to think of my father. I thought of how we had been at odds with each other most of my growing-up years. I knew it was not unusual for a teenager to have conflict with his parents. That was normal enough. But my conflict with my dad seemed much more critical than the norm.

I thought back to the earliest years of my life, when my father had been a struggling law student. Those were the post-Depression years, and he studied long and hard, as well as working to help make ends meet. He had very little time to spend with me, and by the time I entered the first grade I hardly knew him. As a result, the major influence in my life was my mother, whom I adored.

As the years flew by and I grew older, I became afraid of my dad. When he raised his voice at my mother or me, something in me shuddered. This fear turned to hostility in my teenage years. My friends' fathers seemed to care about the things they did and the awards they received, but my own father, I thought, was so caught up in his own interests that he didn't care what happened to me. I knew he loved his work, but I felt insignificant to him.

In later years my hostility turned to a subtle rebellion. I thought, "You go your way, and I'll go mine. You don't bother me, and I won't bother you." If Dad yelled at me, I wished I could yell back. If he ignored me, I ignored him. If he hurt my feelings, I'd try to hurt his. I wanted to give him what I thought he deserved.

I thought of how little communication we had and how he seemed to be able only to express his love for me by giving material things. I didn't feel his love and wondered if it really existed.

I was waiting all those years for him to love me in the way that I wanted to be loved. He never did, so my hate and resentment grew.

Then I heard the message on God's love. If God is love, and I Corinthians 13 describes God's love, then it meant that,

> God's love toward my dad is kind,
> God's love toward my dad is patient,
> God's love toward my dad is not provoked,
> God's love toward my dad does not take into
>   account wrongs suffered,
> God's love toward my dad would bear all things,
>   believe all things,
>   hope all things,
>   endure all things.
> God's love toward my dad would never fail.

I thought, "If God loves my father just the way he is, who am I not to love him also?" My love had been conditional, based on his performance. I had been waiting for him to change. Then, if he changed, I would begin to love him.

My love had said, "Daddy, I'll love you *if* you do this and *if* you do that." Yet God's love simply said, "I love you, period."

No "if's" about it.

It was as though God were saying to me,

> "I love you just the way you are . . .
> I love him just the way he is . . .
> I want you to love him just the way he is . . . "

Tears began streaming down my face as I drove up the mountain road to my home. For the first time in my life I decided to accept my father just as he was. As I reflected on his background and childhood, I was able to see that he had only given to me out of what had been given to him.

Dad was an only child, raised in a small town north of Shreveport, Louisiana. His parents began having marital difficulty early in his life and soon separated and divorced. He stayed with his mother. She died when he was 13 years old, a great loss to a little boy.

Dad went to live with an aunt and uncle. In the meantime, his father was away most of the time dabbling in oil and investments, making and losing tens of thousands of dollars. He rarely expressed love for his son verbally or emotionally, but he did so materially—demonstrating his care by buying his son gifts and taking him on occasional trips. I could see this pattern repeated years later in the way my father related to his own family.

On the other hand, my mother was the youngest of four daughters, raised on a wheat farm in the small community of Jet, near the Oklahoma panhandle, where her parents had pioneered the land. Her family was characterized by love and closeness, sharing together such activities as daily farm chores, recreation, harvesting and attending church.

My mother's family was emotionally and verbally expressive of their appreciation for one another, demonstrating love through many acts of kindness, and hugs and kisses. And this pattern carried through to Mother's raising of her own family. She kept detailed diaries of my first three years of life, up until my twin brother and sister were born—what I did, words I spoke, what I ate and how much I weighed. She was always available to take me anywhere I needed to go, and always ready with words of encouragement for my achievements, however small.

As a child, I had computed these many differences between my parents as meaning, "Mother loves me and Daddy doesn't." But now I could see that they both loved me as best they knew how, in light of their particular backgrounds.

I was grateful for this new understanding as I pulled the car into my driveway. It seemed as if the Lord had done something new in my life. But I knew the real test was yet to come.

Two months later I flew home to Louisiana for vacation, still filled with an attitude of love and acceptance for my dad. I found I was free from judging him, criticizing him, or expressing disapproval either verbally or non-verbally.

I remember one day in particular. We were sitting in the living room together. I was on the couch, and Daddy was in his reclining chair in front of the TV. Soon he fell asleep. I looked over at him in his chair for a long time and then said in a soft whisper,

"Daddy, I love you and I accept you just
    like you are . . . sitting there in your chair."

Over the next days, a strange thing began to happen. As he felt my acceptance, he began to respond with warmth toward me. He seemed to be more caring and sensitive to little things he could do for me. For example, he went to the doctor's office with me when I had to have minor surgery. He waited for me and bought the prescribed medicine at the nearby pharmacy. There was a dress shop near his law office. He brought home three dresses on approval for me to choose which ones I would like to keep.

God was beginning to restore our relationship!

Soon I began to run across verses in Scripture that spoke of parents and of their children's relationships to them. "He chooses our inheritance for us"[2] and wove us while we were in our "mother's womb."[3]

And "For this reason, I bow my knees before the Father, from whom every family in heaven and earth derives its name."[4] God had chosen my parents for me! He was not surprised that I was born into my particular family. When I realized this truth, I thanked God for my parents for the first time in my life.

It wasn't until several years later that I ran across this verse in Ephesians, "Honor your father and mother (which is the first commandment with a promise) that it may be well with you, and that you may live long on the earth."[5] I discovered that the word "honor" means "to count precious, to prize, to value."

I prayed, "Lord, will You show me how to honor my parents? I really want to. Will You give me creativity and show me what to do?"

The Lord answered my prayer in definite ways.

Usually when I went home for a visit, I ran around to see all my friends and spent very little time at home. One of the first thoughts that came to me in answer to my prayer was that, when I went home next, I should spend some time at home, giving myself to my parents in some way before I started visiting other friends.

Soon after my arrival for one visit, I noticed my mother and dad's bedroom furniture, though perfectly good, had nearly 20 years of wear and tear. "Wouldn't it be great to re-do their bedroom furniture?" I thought.

They gave me their permission to begin. I sanded down the bed, the dressers, the night stand, the bookcase. I painted the furniture an antique avocado green. Mother and I found some beautiful fabric and re-covered their headboard and made matching decorator pillows. It was quite a success, and they couldn't get over the fact that I had given four or five days to a project—just for them.

I also thought, "When was the last time I gave my parents a present for no reason . . . just to say 'I love you, and I'm thinking of you?'" I couldn't remember the last time. We usually exchanged gifts on birthdays and Christmas. But my excitement over getting them gifts for no reason at all began to grow.

My parents have always loved to cook. So, following my desire to get them a special surprise, I stopped at a roadside vegetable stand and bought a huge grocery bag full of black-eyed peas. With Mother and Dad watching, almost awe-struck, I sat in the living room shelling peas for hours. They were delighted with the gift, and my father, who is an excellent cook, seemed to take unusual pleasure in specially preparing them for us to eat.

Another time, while visiting the University of Missouri campus in Columbia, I was walking by some shops one morning on the way to the student union building. An item in a jewelry store window caught my eye. It was a silver necklace with the letters ALBERTA engraved in sterling. My mother's name!

I went inside the shop.

"How much is that necklace in the window—the silver one, over on the far right?" I asked. The saleslady behind the counter said, "Well, it's so much per letter and takes approximately six weeks for delivery."

"I don't want to order one," I replied. "I'd like the one in the window—my mother's name is Alberta."

The saleswoman seemed a little surprised. "*My* name is Alberta! The company wanted to make a sample necklace, so I gave them my name to engrave. But I suppose I could sell it to you." Needless to say, my mother loved her unique gift.

My father's hobby is fishing, and our family has always enjoyed fishing trips to nearby lakes. Once, when he and I went fishing I took a picture of him holding a very tiny fish he had caught, a big grin on his round, Jackie Gleason-Lou Costello-type face. I had the picture enlarged, framed and sent to his law office as a surprise. Delighted, Daddy took it over to the courthouse to show some of his colleagues. It remains in a prominent place in his office today.

Sometime later I had to make a major career decision. The thought came to me, "Would I be willing to go to my father and seek his advice?" I also wanted to ask his forgiveness for some of my actions and bad attitudes of years gone by. We had never talked much about personal things, so it was a bit scary to me.

One Sunday afternoon when I was visiting my family, Dad and I were at home alone watching a football game together. I mustered up all the courage I could. Then I asked him for counsel on my career decision. He was extremely helpful, and it went much easier than I expected.

Then I said, "Daddy, there's something else I've been thinking about. I harbored a lot of bad attitudes when I was growing up, attitudes of ungratefulness and lack of love. I realize how wrong I was, and I'd like to ask you to forgive me. Will you forgive me?"

He turned in his great overstuffed reclining chair and looked at me with a slight twinkle in his eyes.

"No." Then he paused. "I don't remember all those things . . . except for the time . . . " He named an instance and laughed.

I thought a moment and said, "Well, will you forgive me for the things you can remember?"

"Yes," he answered.

The ball game continued.

I discussed with him my invitation to accompany Hal Lindsey on his first guided tour to Israel. What did he think?

He replied in Archie Bunker fashion, "I wouldn't give you a nickel for the wailing wall. But if you want to go, it's o.k. with me."

Then I said, "Daddy, I think I'll drive back to Dallas and listen to the rest of the game on the radio."

"Fine," he said. "That's a good idea. You'll beat some of the traffic."

We got up out of our chairs. "Now, where are you going on your next trip?" He had never asked me that before.

"Houston and Nacogdoches," I replied.

"Why don't you warm up one of those cheeseburgers from last night to eat on the way back?" he asked.

I wasn't sure how hungry I was for a leftover cheeseburger, but I wasn't about to turn it down. "Good idea!" I said.

I gathered my things together to leave. At the door, Daddy handed me the cheeseburger and asked, "When will you be home next?" He had never asked me that before, either.

"Oh, about the 21st or 22nd."

Smiling, he said, "I'll see you on the 21st."

A couple of days later I talked to my mother on the phone. "Did Daddy say anything to you about our visit?" I asked.

"Yes, he said, 'Ney must be losing her mind! She asked me for some advice.'"

Some time later I ran across a passage in Proverbs that I thought about for a long time.

> "Hear, my son, your father's instruction,
>   And do not forsake your mother's teaching;
>   Indeed, they are a graceful wreath to your head,
>   And ornaments about your neck."[6]

My parents had never sat me down and conducted a "teaching" or "instruction" session with me, as such. And yet, as I thought about the passage, I realized that they had actually instructed me by things I had seen them do, by living life, by demonstrating things to me. I began writing down on a legal pad things I had learned from my parents, things that I appreciated about them, and qualities they had helped build into my life.

My thoughts evolved into a five-page letter which I sent to my folks on their wedding anniversary. The letter contained the kinds of things I might wish someday I had said to them. When Mother and Dad received my letter, it touched them so deeply that they sat down on the bed and cried.

Parents need and want to know that we, as their children, appreciate all they have done through the years. They need to know that their children have grateful spirits, that they have worth in our eyes, and that we value their counsel and accept them as they are, though they may be different from us.

I am convinced that God wants to heal broken or strained relationships—ones filled with tension and lacking in love. Though my father has never asked me to forgive him of anything, the Lord asked that of me. Today I love and appreciate my dad with all my heart.

And now that the hostility in my own heart has been dealt with, I am better able to see his many wonderful qualities to which I had previously been blind. He is dear, funny and thoughtful. My friends love him and think he is a marvelous story-teller. He is also a gifted lawyer—and a great man in my eyes. I'm very proud of him.

I was thinking recently that, in many ways, my father hasn't changed. But I have. And that's made all the difference.

6

A Brick at a Time

Relationships are "crucibles" of life. They can be full of pain or blessing. They can be the hardest things or the best things in our lives. And many times they are a mixture of both the heights and depths, at one time being a source of supreme joy; at another, excessive sorrow.

In 1969 I found myself in a relationship that would prove to be one of the most significant of my life.

After six years of managing Campus Crusade's personnel department, I assumed the responsibility of a traveling representative to college campuses throughout the south-central states. My job was to meet with staff women at various schools and provide them with spiritual leadership and training. Although traveling representatives normally traveled alone, I requested to be part of a team. That request was honored, and Jean Pietsch and I became partners.

Because we would be working so closely together, Jean and I decided to share an apartment. Our roommate arrangement started out beautifully.

We sat down to go over our personal likes, dislikes and preferences—something I like to call "preventative maintenance." The company which manufactures my car had a program with the same name, encouraging owners to bring in their cars periodically in order to catch problems before they happened.

I had always found this practice, in principle, to be extremely profitable in new living situations. I learned, for in-

stance, that Jean was a meticulous housekeeper, and she wanted
things as neat and tidy as possible. And Jean learned that my
greatest annoyance in life is the sound of chewing gum popping.
It affects me much like chalk screeching across a blackboard!
I hated the fact that gum-smacking bothered me so much, but
Jean resolved to honor that, as I determined to respect her
preferences.

My philosophy, from past experience, had become, "If you
take care of things a brick at a time, you'll never build a wall
between yourself and someone else." I had also found the con-
verse of that statement to be true: if two people don't take
care of problems "a brick at a time," they will build a wall.
And the wall will either remain there forever or come crashing
down in some traumatic way. Both alternatives can be equally
painful.

So Jean and I committed ourselves to a "walls-down, roof-
off" relationship of transparency and openness. We determined
to "walk in the light" with the Lord and with one another, to
communicate with one another whether we felt like it or not.

And we became committed to prayer, both with and for
each other. Our home base was Dallas, Texas, and as soon as
we arrived there, we knelt together and prayed, "Lord, we are
Yours. We commit ourselves to You and to each other, for You
to do in and through us all that You desire. Whatever happens,
Father, don't let us fall short of experiencing the fullness of
Your purposes."

We asked God to make our relationship a reflection of
Christ's prayer in John 17, in which He asked the Father
that we who are believers might be perfected in unity, becoming
one even as Christ and the Father are one.

In my mind, unity or "oneness" did not mean that we
had to be identical people, alike in every way. Rather it meant
that we would not allow conflicts, hostilities and resentments
to be sustained and serve as bricks for "wall construction."
We would be different, but there should be harmony in our
relationship, just as musical instruments can blend together

although they come in every variety.

So we established our relationship on those firm foundations of God's Word, prayer and commitment to communicate. But we knew very little about our varied backgrounds and emotional make-up.

As the first days went on, I found myself feeling increasingly uncomfortable around Jean. There seemed to be a coldness in her manner, a strange combination of hostility and indifference. She didn't express these things so much verbally as she did in attitudes that seemed to come from within, from her spirit.

I knew that Jean was a very gifted person and for much of her life had been by her own description a "loner." It seemed that because of her talents and abilities she always rose to the top too quickly to establish equal relationships with those around her, and she always found herself in leadership positions over them. I would discover later that our friendship provided Jean with her first sustained peer relationship, one in which she had to work out personal problems with someone on a consistent basis.

I tried to understand Jean's behavior in light of her background, but I still found myself at a loss in knowing exactly how to respond to the situation. I had always been a "people-person." Throughout high school and college I majored more in people than in my studies. I savored each opportunity to know and enjoy all kinds of people, and now it seemed the brick wall we had determined not to build was under construction.

Because of our differences in background and personality, our greatest source of frustration seemed to be the way in which we each approached communication. In spite of our commitment to one another and evidence of some progress in mutual understanding, these differences became wearing on both of us over a period of time. Jean seemed continually threatened by my openness in expressing feelings and reactions, and often would withdraw simply out of retaliation. In turn, I sometimes would become hurt and discouraged.

On days when tension seemed literally to fill the air of our Dallas apartment, I would take a break to a neighborhood coffee shop. Often I sat there for what seemed like a very long time, staring out the coffee shop window.

"How did I get myself into this mess?" I would think. "Living with someone who seems so hostile, so cold, so controlled and unfeeling."

My frequent retreats to the coffee shop became a means of regaining a balance of perspective. Because of our difficulties I was finding it easy to question the wisdom and sovereignty of God in His placing Jean and me together. I was tempted to indulge myself in thinking, "We just can't expect to get along because we are so different."

But when I could get away from home and think, I would remember that what God's Word said of His love and acceptance of me and of Jean should be my frame of reference, not what I was experiencing at home.

I thought of Jesus' words when He exposes Satan as the one who "comes only to steal, kill and destroy"[1] the abundant life Christ has provided for us. As I would sit there in the coffee shop, God's perspective flooded my mind. He had called Jean and me together. It was His doing. And since Jesus had prayed for our oneness, it could only be Satan who was out to destroy it. I needed to look past Jean, to the Lord Himself.

I would finish my coffee and head back to the apartment, feeling a little better.

On one occasion, as I came in the front door, Jean looked up. "How was your outing?" she asked.

"Fine," I answered. "I ran some errands and then went to the coffee shop."

"You really like that place, don't you?"

I paused. "Yes, I do. It's a good place to collect my thoughts."

Then I said, "Jean, did you feel the tension in the air that I felt when I left?"

"Yes, I did," she replied.

"Do you know what caused it?"

Jean paused this time, pensive and thoughtful. "No, Ney, I don't know exactly where my feelings come from. Can we pray about it . . . again?"

And so we repeated a practice that would prove to be the glue holding our relationship together over the next three intense, important years. We knelt beside the living room couch and prayed.

"Lord, we don't particularly feel like praying, but here we are. Your Word says we should always pray and not faint.[2] And we feel like fainting, so we'd better pray! Your Word also says, 'In everything give thanks, for this is the will of God in Christ Jesus'[3] concerning us. So while we are *in* this, we choose with our wills to thank You for what we are going through together, even though we don't fully understand our struggles.

"Thank You for Your promise that all things, including this, will work together for good to those who love You, and we do, and who are called according to Your purpose, and we are.[4] You've also said that in You there is no darkness at all,[5] so we ask You to shed light on our paths, and give us wisdom and understanding.

"We claim Your victory over Satan in our lives. We pray for the oneness You want us to have. And, Lord, Your Word says that we are in the process of being conformed to the image of Christ.[6] We ask You now not to stop with us until You are finished. Even though it is painful, we want You to carry on Your work in our lives to accomplish Your purpose."

As in other instances, the tension dissolved and a spirit of unity returned when we prayed aloud together. Jean and I knew how different we were emotionally. But when we couldn't meet on any other level, we knew we could meet on Jesus Christ. We could meet at the foot of the cross. We could meet spiritually in prayer, and we did, hundreds of times while we were together.

Sometimes our differences came out in the mundane, practical experiences of everyday life. For instance, for 45 years, my father has taken coffee into my mother while she is still in bed—a thoughtful gesture to help her begin her mornings. And when I'm home visiting, my parents usually bring coffee in to me in the mornings.

So I started bringing Jean her coffee every morning. But one morning I noticed that, rather than being glad about it, she seemed extremely tense and uncomfortable.

I paused, puzzled. "Maybe I'm doing the wrong thing," I thought to myself. A knot began to form in my stomach. I knew we needed to talk.

Later I asked, "Jean, would you rather I not bring you coffee every morning?" As we discussed it, Jean said, "Ney, I think I'm embarrassed and uncomfortable because I didn't think of doing it first!

"I feel unworthy of receiving your act of kindness—because I had not thought of doing it for you, which also makes me unable to thank you for it."

Years later, Jean reflected back on our "coffee incident." "Your simple gesture was just the beginning of innumerable incidents revealing just how insecure and proud I was. I had the mistaken idea that I had to know everything, think of everything, and do everything or I was unworthy! I put myself under a lot of pressure, didn't I?"

Our first trip together as traveling representatives took us to Lubbock, Texas. One morning we went to the grocery store to buy some things for breakfast. As we were looking over the frozen orange juice selection I asked, "Which kind would you like?"

Jean immediately tensed and seemed completely unable to answer my question directly. That familiar knot began forming in my stomach. I could almost feel another brick being laid, another wall going up. I asked later if we could talk about what happened at the grocery store.

Jean answered, "Well, once again, I was uncomfortable with your thoughtfulness. I would have expected you to choose the juice without asking my opinion. I'm just not used to such detailed concern and care."

"Jean, I don't want to be a pressure to you, but I do care about your feelings and preferences."

She replied, "God is the one who chooses to let us be a pressure on other people, Ney. And He is able to take the pressure off whenever He chooses. In the meantime, we can ride it out and hopefully benefit from it, so please, don't stop expressing that thoughtfulness to me. It's helping me break down some barriers inside."

Another time, I had to learn to be on the receiving end. Because of moving and settling-in expenses, I had an extremely dry spell financially. When my paycheck would come, it would already be spoken for, with little left over even for the bare necessities.

Never before had I needed to be dependent on anyone to borrow such things as shampoo, hair spray—even scotch tape. I hated to borrow from Jean, but I thought there was little choice.

I sensed, however, that it was as hard on her to give to me as it was for me to borrow, which made the situation difficult for both of us.

One day I said, "Jean, I really hate to have to ask you for these things, but I don't know what else I can do. And my asking seems to be hard on you."

I learned from her reply that, having grown up with three sisters who each had their own things, she rarely had to share personal items—and that philosophy had carried over into her roommate relationships.

"I know I'm being selfish. I think the Lord is wanting to teach me to be more giving," she said.

I said, "Well, it's easy for me to give, but very difficult for me to receive! God must be wanting to teach me to receive."

We were able to laugh together, realizing God's providence in teaching us opposite principles through the same situation.

Whatever the circumstances, we found thousands of opportunities either to allow bricks to build into walls or to deal with those barriers day by day, one at a time. One of the most effective ways we found to communicate objectively was to put each issue or "brick" on an invisible table between us. Jean would share with me her perspective of a particular incident, then I would do the same.

We discovered that we normally approached the same thing from totally opposite directions, but the more frequently we discussed our perspectives, the greater our understanding of one another became.

Sometimes we would express an insight gained just through talking things out. Or if need be, we would ask the other person's forgiveness. There were times we could not come to an understanding, so we would simply agree to leave the issue on the "table."

Often it helped to gain objectivity by each of us asking, "Is this conflict like any others I've had previously?" Some reactions spring from similar experiences in the past rather than just the present situation. A clue to know whether this is the case is if we find ourselves reacting far beyond the reality of the present situation.

Once, when we discussed this question, we discovered that I reminded Jean in some ways of other people she had known, whom she had resented because of their freedom, for instance, to be emotionally expressive. So some of our insights helped bring understanding and healing to those relationships.

We found that another "brick" was something I've come to call a "vain imagination balloon." A vain imagination can occur when: 1) I *think* you're thinking something negative about me; or 2) you *think* I'm thinking something negative about you. Usually a vain imagination has no firm basis in reality—in other words, the thought hasn't been verbalized, and it is not a known fact. For example, someone might think,

> "I don't think she likes me."
> "He wishes I would leave."
> "She doesn't like my hair."
> "He thinks I'm not dressed properly."

We imagine those thoughts to be true, and so they begin to "balloon" in our minds, floating in and out to chip away at our relationships.

Vain imaginations can be very destructive. Many relationships have been totally destroyed simply because the individuals involved believed their imaginations without checking them out to see if they were true.

Whenever they would arise between Jean and me, which they often did, we determined to discuss them openly. Because we verbalized our imaginings, we were able to put needles in our "balloons"—and they disappeared!

We had the opportunity to deflate a balloon during a visit to Kansas University. One afternoon we were preparing for some evangelistic meetings in a sorority house. My heart was very heavy because I felt, according to Jean's behavior that day, she really didn't want to be around anyone, especially me. I thought to myself, "I just can't go into those meetings until I've talked it over with her."

Just before it was time to go, I mustered up the courage to talk to her about my impressions.

"Jean," I asked, "can we talk before we go?"

She looked up from her book and said, "Sure."

I continued, "I have a strong feeling that you don't want to go to this meeting with me tonight."

She exclaimed, "Oh, no, Ney! That never occurred to me. But I was thinking that you didn't want to go to the meeting with *me!*"

"Jean, I promise, that never even occurred to me!" We were both visibly relieved, knowing that Satan was truly at work to kill, steal and destroy our unity, especially when we were about to minister together as speakers in the meetings.

Another problem that often arises in relationships with others is that of wrong expectations. We can come to demand more of people than they are capable of giving or begin simply to take them for granted.

I once heard the story of a man who decided to try an

experiment for one month. In this experiment, he planned to go up and down a certain neighborhood block and give away $100 bills to each household as a gift, with no strings attached.

The first day of his experiment, as he went from house to house, the residents seemed extremely suspicious—of his sanity. They would hesitantly reach from behind their screen doors and take the bills with a jerk. Their reactions were similar on the second day of his rounds.

But by the third and fourth days, many of the people had cashed the bills and found them to be the real thing. The neighborhood was buzzing with the news of these daily gifts of $100 bills.

The second week people were actually waiting on their front porches, peering down the street to watch for the man to come. They began visiting with one another, shouting in neighborly fashion across yards and the street.

By the third week, however, the novelty of the man's visits seemed to be wearing off. The residents seemed to take on a humdrum approach to the daily gifts. The gifts were becoming "old hat." And by the fourth week, since the pattern of visits had become firmly established, they were considered an accepted part of everyday neighborhood life.

On the last day of the month the man tried a different approach. He decided to walk down the street again, but with no money at all to give away. As he did so a strange phenomenon occurred. Residents threw open their doors, stepped out on their porches and shouted angrily, "Where's our money?" And, "You so-and-so, how dare you not give me my $100 today?"

What had happened? The people had come to demand and expect something that was originally presented to them as an unmerited gift. They had grown to feel that the man "owed" them the $100 bills.

This is an example of how we can be with other people and with the Lord. All of life starts out as a gift—our families, our friends, our material possessions, our health. As life goes on, we can begin to take those gifts for granted and develop expectations of how things are "supposed" to be. If and when they are withdrawn, we may then become angry or demanding because we think we have a "right" to them. Instead, it is helpful if we determine to be grateful for whatever is given to us.

Romans 15:7 beautifully expresses the principle of accepting others. "Wherefore, accept one another, just as Christ also accepted us to the glory of God." It is actually glorifying to God when we accept one another, and it brings dishonor to Him when we don't.

If we do not choose with our wills to accept others, then all our hopes become placed in the demand that they perform according to our wishes. If others meet our expectations, we usually have few problems with them. But when they don't perform up to our "par," then we tend to lower the boom on them, becoming judgmental in attitude and letting them know in various ways that they have, indeed, fallen short of our standards. And that is when others begin to feel they are failures in our eyes.

David writes in Psalms 62 that his hopes and expectations were in God alone. Why? Because God is the only "constant" in life, and everything else is variable. If we put our hopes in variables, we'll invariably be disappointed.

Many times I had to ask myself, "Where have I placed my hopes? In Jean's performance or in the Lord?" If we plant our hopes in another person's performance, or even our own, our lives will become a roller coaster ride, simply because performances go up and down.

Though all of these things—individual differences, vain imaginations and wrong expectations—contribute to problems in relationships, perhaps the most destructive force of all is that of *hurt*. There were times when the differences between Jean and me caused tremendous hurt.

I remember vividly one evening when Jean was not home. I knelt beside my bed, crying out in prayer, "Lord, I don't feel like Jean loves me, and I don't feel any love for Jean. After all these years I thought I knew something about love but I'm not sure I really know a thing about it!

"I pray that You would teach me about Your love. I've run out of mine. I yield my body to You as an instrument of righteousness. I pray that I can be to Jean what she needs in You, and only You know what that is. By Your Spirit, please do for me and through me what I cannot do for myself."

I knew that both of our hearts were right and that we both loved the Lord. We were different, but different didn't mean "wrong." But when I was hurt by those differences, I responded in a variety of ways.

My first tendency was to blame Jean or find fault with her. I would think to myself, "If it weren't for Jean, everything would be all right." But then I would take hold of my thoughts and choose with my will not to blame Jean. I had to take personal responsibility for my behavior and for the negative attitudes that surfaced in my heart.

For example, I prayed, "Lord, what qualities are You wanting to build into my life through this experience?" Since I was finding it difficult to love, the answer that came to mind was "love."

As I began to dwell on I Corinthians 13, I was once again reminded, as in my experiences with my father, that God's kind of love has a lot more to do with the will than it does with feelings or emotions.

When we see something we don't like in other people, our tendency is to judge them, zeroing in on what we don't like about them, blaming them for being as they are. But God's desire is that we not judge others. He sees the beginning and the end. He knows where we each have come from, and He sees all the hurt we've experienced.

Once a little boy and his father were riding together on a train. All day long the boy sniffed and whined and cried intermittently. When night fell, the boy and his father retired to a sleeping berth on the train. But the boy's sobbing could be heard through the curtains.

A fellow passenger, who had been hearing the little boy's crying for hours, became impatient and irritated. In disgust, he jumped from his berth to the floor and threw back the curtains where father and son were settled in for the night.

He said harshly, "Mister, if you can't control this boy and make him stop crying, you need to let his mother handle him."

The father replied softly, "Sir, his mother has just passed away. We are taking her home to be buried."

The observer had seen part of the truth and judged the whole, based on his partial information. When he gained additional information, he could understand the behavior.

In the same way, as I was able to open my eyes to see the total picture of Jean's life and background, I found freedom from judgmental attitudes.

Another response we often have when we are hurt is the desire to hurt back. This "vengeance syndrome" can destroy any relationship. But I Peter 3:8,9 says, "To sum up, let all be harmonious, sympathetic, brotherly, kindhearted, and humble in spirit, not returning evil for evil, or insult for insult, but giving a blessing instead." We need to practice giving a blessing when we've been hurt.

One way of giving a blessing is to "sow good seed" into the life of someone who has hurt us. I once had a garden, and I discovered that when I planted a cucumber seed, for example, the crop didn't yield just one cucumber, but many cucumbers would spring from the one tiny seed. Not only that, but if I planted cucumber seeds, I reaped cucumbers, not carrots. I got exactly what I sowed, and even more than I sowed.

I have often heard the expression "you reap what you sow" in the context of doing bad things which reap bad consequences. However, the statement also holds true in the context of doing good things which reap good consequences.

Sowing bad seeds can reap difficulties, but sowing good seeds can reap love and harmony. Galatians 6:7-9 says, "Do not be deceived, God is not mocked; for *whatever a man sows this he will also reap.* For the one who sows to his own flesh shall from the flesh reap corruption, *but* the one who sows to the Spirit shall from the Spirit reap eternal life. *And let us not lose heart in doing good, for in due time we shall reap if we do not grow weary"* [italics mine].

And James 3:18 indicates that if we want to make peace, we must sow righteous seed. What is righteous seed? It is the fruit of the Spirit; it is Christ-like behavior and a Christ-like response to any given situation.

The fruit of the Spirit is described in Galatians as "love, joy, peace, patience, kindness, goodness, faithfulness, gentleness, self-control; against such things there is no law."[7] That means we can be as loving, kind, patient and good as we want to be, because there's no law against it!

When someone sends a "hate seed" my way, I can let it take root and grow a larger crop of hatred and then throw it back into the other person's life, producing more hate seeds, building resentment and bitterness. Or when the hate seed comes my way, I can acknowledge it for what it is, but choose to break the cycle by forgiving and doing good to the other person.

Jean and I endeavored, as best we knew how, to sow good seed into one another's lives. Our first year together was by far our most difficult, filled with the greatest misunderstanding. Yet it was during that year that I secretly saved mementos from each one of our trips. I saved postcards, souvenirs and pictures and kept a log of our ministry for the year. At the end of the year, I put it all together in a large scrapbook and surprised her with it.

On the other hand, Jean would often make our airline reservations, cook great meals for us, and write or phone ahead to make arrangements for our trips. Emotionally, there were times when neither of us felt like doing "nice" things for one another. But these were ways in which we determined to sow good seed into each other's lives.

Perhaps the greatest healing response to hurt, however, is forgiveness. I decided to choose with my will to forgive Jean whenever I experienced hurt. I had to practice forgiveness over and over again. One thing that helped was to break down the word "forgive" and ask,

Am I looking *for* a way of *giving* to Jean?
or
Am I withholding?

If I found myself withholding in my heart, chances were that I really didn't have an attitude of forgiveness, and I wasn't looking for ways of giving.

Another question I've asked myself is,

"Is my God bigger than my hurt?"

I am the one to choose whether to allow God to loom larger in my eyes than the hurt I've experienced. Or I can allow the hurt to become the all-consuming issue in my life, so that it becomes impossible to see God in the situation. It is often a difficult thing to choose to see God as being larger than my hurt, but ultimately it is the right choice, as it was the right choice for me in my relationship with Jean.

In our three years together we traveled the states of Texas, Louisiana, Oklahoma, Kansas, Missouri, Nebraska, Colorado and Wyoming. We spoke hundreds of times, saw people come to know Christ as Savior and saw many lives changed. Because we chose to honor the Lord, and each other, I believe God used us as a team in many special ways.

Jean and I lived together, ate, ministered, entertained and worked through problems together. As time passed, we began to catch glimpses of true oneness.

The psalmist wrote, " . . . How good and pleasant it is for the brethren to dwell together in unity!"[8] Those "good and pleasant" times became more and more frequent toward the end of our third year. We actually began to enjoy one another! We felt that the Lord had honored our heart attitudes and prayers, our communication and our commitment to working things through. In our minds, He had performed a miracle. We grew to miss each other when we were apart, rather than being glad for the relief from pressure.

The summer of our third year Jean returned from her family home in Houston and exclaimed, "Ney, do you remember me once mentioning someone named Doug? I knew him four years ago—and didn't like him very much?"

"Yes," I said, "I recall your telling me about him."

"Well, when I was home, I ran into him, and he asked me out to dinner. After dinner we drove to Galveston, sat on the beach one balmy evening and visited for a long time. He's really changed since I knew him before. I *really* enjoyed being with him—which surprised me!"

Two months later, Doug phoned Jean from Illinois to say he was coming to Dallas for a conference. They attended the conference together every day. When meetings weren't scheduled, they would visit, shop or go sightseeing.

When Doug left to go home, Jean said, "Ney, I feel like a part of me is gone." The next thing I knew they were writing back and forth, then phoning back and forth, then flying back and forth. I wasn't surprised when they became engaged in November.

One evening I received an unexpected phone call from Doug. "Ney, Jean and I have been talking, and I want you to know that we realize we could not be getting married apart from the things you two learned and worked through in your three years together. I want to thank you personally for your investment in Jean's life."

The call touched me deeply, and I cried grateful, happy tears that night for all that the Lord had done. The last month before Jean left to be married, I could not mention her name without tears coming to my eyes. We had shared so much in those years, and I knew I would miss her deeply.

I could see more clearly then that the sensitivity I had originally thought lacking in Jean's life was there all the time. In fact, I marveled at the depth of her compassion and love.

But it took all we experienced to bring it out.

Jean wrote me recently and said, "The experiences we had together have *everything* to do with my having a happy marriage. As you continued to love me, the walls of fear and hostility gradually began to crumble! After I learned to accept my own feelings of failure, fear and depression, I could be patient and understanding of Doug's feelings, too.

"Dating," she continued, "could not have prepared me for marriage. I was too guarded about my true feelings. I needed to live with someone who would confront me with the truth about myself and about herself."

It has occurred to me, as a result of my experiences in relating to people, that though it is almost easy to love God because He is perfect, it's not so easy to love one another—because we're not perfect! That must account for Jesus' statement that the world would know that He is God by our love for one another. It is not natural, but supernatural, for us to love one another with the kind of love and commitment that stays in there when feelings are saying, "I want out!" For Jean and me, the blessings came in the "staying in," not in the "getting out."

During my years with Jean I learned that to reject an office-mate, roommate, husband or wife is to reject God's provision, because God has sovereignly placed you together. Not only did I learn to take care of things a "brick at a time," but I learned to pray when I didn't feel like it and to communicate when I didn't want to. I also learned invaluable lessons in dealing with vain imaginations and hurt.

If Jean Pietsch and I had allowed all the potential walls to build up, we might have ended up hating each other, and God would not have allowed our ministry to flourish as He did. Although in many ways we were opposites, we saw the Lord bring us together in oneness and harmony; the love, commitment, gratefulness and devotion we have in our hearts toward one another is powerful to this day.

7

Unmasking the Enemy

When Jean and I first met Jackie Hudson, she was working in an office in Dallas, Texas, helping with preparations for EXPLO '72, a conference which would eventually draw over 80,000 Christians to be trained in principles of evangelism and discipleship.

Jackie was just entering Christian work and wanted with all her heart to serve and follow the Lord. She was vivacious and outgoing and the picture of happiness.

When I saw her three months later, the contrast was unbelievable. I was leaving a class to have lunch with a friend when I happened to see Jackie in the back of the classroom. She seemed as though she were off in another world. As I walked toward her and came close enough to see the dark circles under her eyes, I realized that she looked very pale. I wondered if she was well.

"Jackie, you look awful." I was surprised at my own abruptness. "Are you o.k.?"

"No." Her lip began to quiver, and she was on the verge of tears.

I reached out to touch her shoulder. "Do you have a few minutes to talk?"

Jackie nodded, and the tears began to run down her cheeks.

We moved outside to a grassy area on the campus and sat down. "Can you tell me what's wrong?" I asked.

She began, "Well, Ney, this may sound strange, but last

month during EXPLO, I was sitting in the Cotton Bowl (where the evening meetings were held) looking out at those 80,000 people. Some thoughts flashed into my mind. Thoughts like, 'How do I really know there is a God? How do I know all these people aren't just fooling themselves?'"

She paused and took a deep breath.

"I dismissed the thoughts, but in the days that followed, they kept coming back. The more I questioned, the greater my doubts became. Now it's to the point that I don't know for sure about anything."

Jackie shifted positions on the grass, looking down then back at me. "One part of me knows that it's real, but my doubts keep plaguing me, and I feel like I can't believe. I can't believe."

The pitch in her voice raised. "My doubts seem true, and now I'm not even sure I'm a Christian. I haven't been able to sleep or eat. I've lost nine pounds. Sometimes I wonder if Satan has a hand in all this. I can't believe, but I want to . . . I can't . . . " Her voice cracked and she began to sob. " . . . I want to. But I feel like I'm fooling myself."

Together we turned to some Scripture passages on faith, and we began to talk through them. I asked, "What is faith, Jackie?"

"I guess on the basis of what you've said, it's ~~taking~~ God ~~at His Word.~~ But Ney, I don't even know if there is a God, so how can I take Him at His Word?"

Then I explained to Jackie that there was a spiritual battle going on, and Satan had blinded her mind to the truths of Scripture. It seemed appropriate to stop and pray. I prayed that she would be delivered from Satan's power, that God would give her grace to believe Him again. At the conclusion of our time I left a packet of Bible verses with her, encouraging her to spend time thinking through them. We agreed to stay in touch.

The next day, Jackie located me at a friend's home.

"Ney, since I saw you yesterday, I still haven't been able

to sleep or eat. I don't know what to do."

"Do you have a Bible close by?" I asked.

"Yes."

"O.K., turn to I Peter. I know you say you don't believe the Bible right now, but for a few minutes, let's just pretend you do." I asked her to start reading aloud verses six through ten of chapter 5.

She began, "Humble yourselves, therefore, under the mighty hand of God, that He may exalt you at the proper time."

"What does that tell you to do?" I asked.

"Humble myself."

"How do you humble yourself?"

She continued to read. "Casting all your anxiety upon Him, because He cares for you."

"How many anxieties?"

"All."

"And why are you supposed to do that?"

Jackie's voice sounded almost hopeful. "Because He cares for me."

"Yes," I answered. "He cares for you. Now read the next line."

"Be of sober spirit, be on the alert. Your adversary, the devil, prowls about like a roaring lion, seeking someone to devour."

"Now, Jackie, what is God's warning to you?"

"To be on the alert."

"Why?"

"Because the devil is out to get me."

"Who is the devil?"

"He is my adversary."

"O.K., read the next verse."

"But resist him, firm in your faith, knowing that the same experiences of suffering are being accomplished by your brethren who are in the world."

"What does God tell you to do, Jackie?"

"Resist Satan."

"How are you to resist him?"

"By being firm in my faith."

"What is faith?"

"Taking God at His Word."

"And what does the passage say next?"

" . . . Knowing that the same experiences of suffering are being accomplished by your brethren who are in the world."

"Jackie, this means that you aren't alone in this! Other people are going through the same things you are. One of Satan's tricks is to make you think you are all alone.

"In the next verse, God promises, 'And after you have suffered for a little, the God of all grace, who called you to His eternal glory in Christ, will Himself perfect, confirm, strengthen and establish you.' What you are going through won't last forever."

I continued. "I want you to memorize these verses. And since the whole passage is talking about choosing to believe God's truth over Satan's lies, I want you to write in the margin of your Bible these words, 'Choose to believe.'"

We said goodbye and arranged another time to meet.

A couple of days later we met in a restaurant. Again she said, "I desperately want to believe, but I can't."

"Jackie, you have built a pattern of believing the wrong things, and now you need to start building a pattern of believing the right things. You are thinking of yourself as not having faith, but you need to think, 'I am beginning to develop a new habit of walking by faith.'"

As we continued to meet, I felt we made some progress, but I was still very concerned for her. When she left for her staff assignment at Oregon State University, she was still very, very low.

In the days that followed I continued to pray for her and kept updated through a mutual friend.

When I saw Jackie a year later she was the picture of victory again. She told me some of the things she had learned.

"The thing that freed me was realizing I was in a spiritual battle. I began to realize I had an old nature that was hostile toward God and prone to doubt. But I also had a new nature that could respond to God.

"I realized, too, that my will was the key. With my will I could choose to believe God and choose to take Him at His Word regardless of what my feelings or my old nature told me. When I began to get into the habit of believing God, my doubts faded."

It has been five years since my first encounter with Jackie. Today she has one of the most positive, powerful ministries of any young woman I know. The opening line of a recent article about her said, "If Jackie Hudson were to launch her own media campaign, her bumper sticker would read, 'Believe God and He'll Do Anything.'"

In the heat of a spiritual battle for her mind and will, the change came when she chose to believe God's Word. She put her trust in God's promise that "greater is He who is in you than he who is in the world."[1]

I was grateful Jackie had taken to heart the counsel that had been given. But if she had sought my counsel a year earlier, I might not have known how to help her in her struggle. It wasn't because I'd never heard of "spiritual warfare," but that I greatly underestimated the power and scope of Satan's influence.

C.S. Lewis wrote that if Satan can get us to disbelieve his existence, he has won a major battle because his activity goes unrecognized. Though I believed in Satan's existence, I often acted as though I didn't. Even as a topic of conversation, it seemed unnecessary, and almost distasteful, to discuss him.

But all that changed during the summer I moved to Dallas from Arrowhead Springs. One day I was in my bedroom, talking aloud to the Lord. I asked Him to "teach me to pray." As I heard my words, I realized that phrase had a familiar ring to it. I remembered that long ago the disciples had asked the same thing of Jesus. I turned to the Lord's Prayer, which was Christ's answer to the disciples' request.

A phrase in the prayer, "And do not lead us into temptation, but deliver us from evil (the evil one),"[2] stood out like a neon sign. I recalled another of Christ's prayers, found in John 17. Jesus was praying to the Father on behalf of believers who would remain on earth after He ascended to heaven. "I do not ask Thee to take them out of the world, but to keep them from the evil one."[3]

I thought, "It's very interesting that these two prayers of Jesus have one thing in common—a request to be delivered or kept from the evil one, Satan." After that I began to pray an almost daily personal prayer that I would be kept from Satan's power. I knew I was praying in agreement with Jesus Christ, who would be interceding for me in heaven for the same thing.

As I began to understand more of Satan and his ways, I asked the Lord to teach me what I should know about spiritual warfare. He led me to Ephesians 6.

> "Finally, be strong in the Lord, and in the strength of His might. Put on the full armor of God, that you may be able to stand firm against the schemes of the devil. For our struggle is not against flesh and blood, but against the rulers, against the powers, against the world forces of this darkness, against the spiritual forces of wickedness in the heavenly places. Therefore, take up the full armor of God, that you may be able to resist in the evil day, and having done everything, to stand firm. Stand firm therefore, having girded your loins with the truth, and having put on the breastplate of righteousness, and having shod your feet with the preparation of the gospel of peace; in addition to all, taking up the shield of faith with which you will be able to extinguish all the flaming missiles of the evil one."[4]

This passage reveals many things about Satan, and among the most important is that he is a deceiver. When someone deceives, he makes something seem like the truth when it is not. Good magicians, for example, have mastered the art of deception.

Satan is exposed in this passage as a deceptive schemer— wily, crafty and deceitful. Jesus called him the "father of lies."[5] His "schemes" take many forms, and his strategies are infinite in their variety. At times he will make an all-out attack; at other times he is subtle.

But Paul also writes that with the shield of faith we can counter his attacks. We can actually extinguish all of Satan's flaming missiles, or "fiery darts," as the King James version puts it.

What are these "fiery darts?" And how can we "take up the shield of faith" to extinguish them? Just as in a war, the enemy has an advantage if he is camouflaged, so Satan has a particular advantage in our lives if his tactics aren't disclosed.

One of Satan's most powerful weapons is his use of *doubt*. There are thousands of Christians in the world who are just like Jackie was, living lives of defeat and despair. Their struggles are rooted in the simple fact that they have stopped believing God. They are choosing to believe their doubt-filled thoughts, rather than the Word of God.

This is one of Satan's ancient but most effective schemes. In the Garden of Eden he approached Eve with the taunting words, "Indeed, has God said . . . ?"[6] Satan's desire was to undermine Eve's trust, confidence and belief in God and His Word. He is doing the same thing today. And he is victorious every time, unless his "victim" chooses to believe God, just as Jackie did.

Another of Satan's tactics is that of a feeling of *condemnation*. There have been times when, out of the blue, I have felt condemned but for no apparent reason.

Satan is referred to in Scripture as "the accuser of the brethren."[7] When he has attacked me with condemnation, I have found some powerful responses to his assaults in Romans 8.

"There *is* therefore *now no* condemnation to those who are in Christ Jesus . . . . If God is for us, who is against us? He who did not spare His own Son, but delivered Him up for us all, how will He not also with Him freely give us all things? Who will bring a charge against God's elect? God is the one who justifies; who is the one who condemns? Christ Jesus is He who died, yes, rather who was raised, who is at the right hand of God, who also intercedes for us"[8] [italics mine].

After reading this passage, I have prayed, "Lord, I feel condemned, but I choose to believe what Your Word says. Thank You that I am not condemned by You." The most effective counterattack for me has been simple affirmation of my faith in God's Word.

(3) One of the most personally destructive of all his strategies is Satan's attempt to make us *feel forsaken by God*. There are times when I've felt very lost and alone. It has seemed like no one cared about what I was going through, and that even God was oblivious to me. Often that feeling has arisen from an emotionally trying situation and has been a natural initial response.

The "evil one's" tactic has been to take that feeling one step further—until I've actually begun believing that not only does no one care about me, but God Himself has withdrawn His love and concern, even to the point of completely giving up on me.

For many people who have experienced the same thing, such feelings have led to desperate, sometimes suicidal, thoughts. When I find my mind veering in this direction, I like to listen to these encouraging words from Romans 8:

"Who shall separate us from the love of Christ? Shall tribulation, or distress, or persecution, or famine, or nakedness, or peril, or sword? . . . But in all these things we overwhelmingly conquer through Him who loved us. For I am convinced that neither death, nor life, nor angels, nor principalities, nor things present nor things to come, nor powers, nor height, nor depth, nor any other created thing, shall be able to separate us from the love of God, which is in Christ Jesus our Lord."[9]

Paul was saying that nothing can separate us from the love of God. In fact, Jesus promised, "I will never desert you, nor will I ever forsake you."[10] The word "never" in English does not adequately convey the force of His statement. In the original language the word used is called a "triple negative," and there is no single-word English equivalent. In essence, He was saying, "I will never, no never, no never leave you nor forsake you."

Another of Satan's "fiery darts" is something closely related to thoughts of being forsaken by God: *a sense of worthlessness.* I once heard someone say that infants still in their mother's arms are constantly receiving love and positive attention. They are told "I love you, you precious little baby." But as the child grows up, various experiences of rejection—from his family or the outside world—may take their toll and completely negate all the positive input he had as a child. As a result, by the time he reaches adulthood, he may feel worthless.

I am convinced that Satan uses anything and everything he can to undermine our sense of personal worth. He hates us, and if he can get us to hate ourselves and believe that we are of no value, especially to God, then he has successfully convinced us to think the exact opposite of God's Word.

Sometimes he aims his "worthlessness" attack toward us just after we have sinned. God loves who we are although He doesn't always love what we do. He deals with us to correct our *behavior,* whereas Satan's tactic is to destroy our *person,* our *character.*

For example, let's suppose you tell a lie. Satan might say, "You liar! You're nothing but a liar, and you know it. You'll never be worth anything."

On the other hand, God's response is, "I love you, but you did not tell the truth. I love you too much to let you continue doing that, so we need to correct that behavior."

God loves us. We are "precious" in His sight![11] In fact, as mind-boggling as it may be, and as hard as it is to comprehend, we are worth as much to God as His own Son. Just as an item in a store is worth what is "given" for it, we are worth what was given for us. If we are worth that much to God, it can only be the adversary himself who tries to make us feel worthless.

When Satan has attacked me in this way, I have prayed, "Lord, I feel worthless. But I thank You that I am worth as much to You as Your own dear Son."

When Satan directs his assaults at us individually, it is only a small part of his ultimate strategy to cripple the effective functioning of the whole body of Christ completely. And sometimes, without our realizing it, the "accuser of the brethren" employs us to do his work for him.

One of his flaming missiles most disruptive to unity is criticism. Since Jesus prayed for our oneness, we know that if there is discord being sown among us it cannot be from God but from the evil one.

If we have ever been hurt by the words of others spoken behind our backs, we know how painful it can be. That pain can motivate us to keep from speaking hurting words of anyone else. Even in the midst of our difficulties, Jean and I committed ourselves to give good reports about one another to other people. There were times when we sought counsel from others about our relationship, but only when we had agreed to do so.

In his book, *My Utmost for His Highest,* Oswald Chambers teaches that discernment is for the purpose of prayer and not for the purpose of fault-finding. Because none of us is perfect, there will inevitably be things in other people's lives that we don't like or with which we don't agree. Some of these observations may be valid; however, when we become negative and judgmental about those things, the result can be momentary spiritual defeat, leading to frustration and worry.

On the other hand, if we take the things about others that are hard to accept and prayerfully give them to the Lord, we are working in cooperation with God, not Satan. We are acknowledging His ability to do what He wants to do in lives and in difficult situations.

There is an attack from the evil one that I like to call the "fiery dart of 'if only.'" This was another technique Satan used on Eve in the garden to persuade her to disobey God and eat of the tree of the knowledge of good and evil.[12]

In essence he said, "Eve, this tree limits you. If only it weren't for this tree you would know everything God knows."

To this day, Satan tries to convince us that we are limited —first by one thing and then another. He speaks in subtle ways, saying, "This person (wife, husband, child, roommate, officemate, relative, parent, etc.) limits you. If only they were not in your life, things would almost be perfect."

When Jean and I lived together, Satan would whisper, "Ney, Jean limits you. If it weren't for her you would be a lot happier, and life would be much better for you." Had I believed Satan, I would have begun acting on my belief and would have lived for the day when we would no longer be roommates.

Yet, I knew I needed to look past Jean and put my hope in the Lord and His Word. As my friend Don Meredith has said, "We need to see the people around us as 'no limitation' to us."

Joseph, in the Old Testament, was hated by his brothers. He was thrown into a pit and sold into slavery. From all outward appearances, he was extremely limited by his circumstances. Joseph could have thought, "If only my brothers hadn't done this, I'd be free!"

Instead he managed to hope in the Lord, Who worked it together for good. Joseph was able to say later that though his brothers meant evil against him, God meant it for good.[13]

After their brother Lazarus had been dead for four days, Mary and Martha came running up to Jesus. Mary said, "Lord, if You had been here, my brother would not have died."[14]

Jesus met their "if" with His "if." He responded, "Did I not say to you, *if you believe, you will see the glory of God?*" [italics mine]. Moments later, Lazarus was resurrected from the dead.

We must believe God for the "if only's" in our lives, for the people or the circumstances we feel are limiting us because He is able to bring glory out of all those things.

Doubt, criticism, feelings of worthlessness, the "if only's," feelings of condemnation—they provide just a sampling of the numberless sinister, devious strategies of the evil one. Satan truly "prowls about like a roaring lion." He seeks to devour us all, and he often does it by hurling one "fiery dart" at a time. The cumulative effect of his attacks can immobilize anyone who does not take up the shield of faith against him.

Such was the case with someone whom I met a few years ago. I had flown to the East Coast to spend time with some staff women there. Barbie Leyden met me at the airport with, "Ney, I am very concerned about Marti. She's just not herself anymore. She is very depressed and seems to have given up on life. Would you spend some time with her?"

The first time we met I could tell almost instantaneously that her will had become completely passive, and that she was not believing God at all. She told me that a particular young man had fallen in love with her, and she had responded wholeheartedly. As she sought God's will as to whether they were to be married, she felt the Lord spoke to her from certain Scriptures confirming that they would marry. She had claimed those Bible verses believing that they supported her hopes that they would get together.

When their relationship didn't develop as she had hoped, she lost all faith and confidence in God and gave up. She just didn't care anymore. She refused to take to heart anything I said, and as we talked further, she became like a "slippery fish," making statements that completely evaded the issue at hand.

When I left our appointment, I realized I hadn't been able

to get through to her in any way. Heavily burdened, I began to
pray fervently for our next time together. I remembered these
words from II Timothy, " . . . With gentleness correcting those
who are in opposition, if perhaps God may grant them repentance leading to the knowledge of the truth, and they may
come to their senses and escape from the snare of the devil,
having been held captive by him to do his will."[16] These verses
seemed to speak to me of this situation.

I said, "Father, I pray You will grant Marti repentance
leading to the knowledge of the truth, and I pray she will
come to her senses and escape from the snare of the devil,
having been held captive by him to do his will. Father, I pray
she will give her will back to You, and there will be new light
and new hope and a new beginning for her."

The next day we met again. I told her I had been thinking
about her since we last talked.

"When you prayed that you would marry that fellow," I
said, "and claimed verses to that effect, and it didn't happen,
you lost confidence in God and His Word, right?"

"That's right," she responded. "I believe God let me down."

"You know, Marti, nowhere in the Bible is there a verse
that says 'so-and-so will be your husband.' God didn't let you
down. You wanted the Bible to say that, and you read that into
some verses, right?"

She agreed.

"Rather than losing confidence in God and His Word, you
need to lose confidence in your reading into His Word something that it doesn't say." She indicated that she hadn't thought
of that before.

Then I told her how dangerous it was for her will to be in
a passive state. I said, "Marti, I'd like to hear you say 'I *want* to
be out of this.'" But once again she seemed to be slipping away
as she began to speak vaguely and evasively.

I shared with her the passage I had recalled from II Timothy.
As I read the verses, she seemed really to hear me for the first
time and grasp a sense of the importance of what was happening

to her.

"I thought God was going to do everything to get me out of this, but I see now that my will needs to be active. I thought God was responsible to get me out of my depressions and downhill trends, but I never knew I had a part until today."

I told her that her part was to take her "mustard seed" of faith[17] and choose to believe God's Word. Because all of her thoughts were of a despairing nature, and they all ended by questioning God, I suggested that she begin keeping a daily journal. In this journal, I encouraged her to pour out onto paper all of her negative, doubtful thoughts and then to end her thought progression with something from God's Word which would speak directly to the feelings she had just expressed. For instance, if her thoughts led her to believe God had forsaken her, she should end the journal page with Jesus' words, "I will never desert you, nor will I ever forsake you."

I told her I knew that in the depths of her heart she wanted to be out of her despondency, but she needed to exercise her will. Then I suggested that we pray together.

"I've prayed so many times, and it doesn't work," she said.

"But I want to enter into this with you," I responded, "and bear your burdens by praying with you. You have thought of yourself as having no faith and as not believing. I want you to think instead, 'I'm beginning to develop a new habit of taking God at His Word.' Give yourself time to develop this new habit. I'll commit myself to pray for you every day for the next two months."

So we prayed together. She told the Lord that she had given her will over to unbelief, and now she wanted to give her will to Him to believe Him and His Word. I prayed for her, I encouraged her to seek prayer support from others, since she hadn't shared with anyone else what she was going through.

Later that day I wrote in my journal, "I believe this could be a turning point in Marti's life. I pray that it will be."

Two days later I called her. She had just spent over three hours in Scripture and was beginning to see how she had been deceived in various ways. "For instance, I was believing that my life was going downhill," she said, "but II Corinthians 3:18 says we are being transformed 'from glory to glory.' Most of all, now I can see the part my will has to play in allowing God to change me."

Marti seemed grateful for my call, and I was pleased to see that she was beginning to form the habit of believing God.

Four years have passed since our encounter, and my friend has not only come out of her despondency completely, but she also has been serving the Lord successfully overseas the past two years.

As Marti discovered, it is vitally important that we keep our wills actively obedient to the truth of Scripture, because Satan is the one who will keep sending flaming missiles and fiery darts to undermine our faith. He will keep coming in many different forms, planting seeds of doubt and unbelief in our hearts and minds any way he can.

But we must also remember that he is a defeated foe. Christ won the battle over Satan on the cross, and as we remember our *position* in Christ, we can operate from that vantage point.

The apostle Paul understood our victorious position. He wrote,

"I pray that the eyes of your heart may be enlightened, so that you may know what is the hope of His calling, what are the riches of the glory of His inheritance in the saints, and what is the surpassing greatness of His power toward us who believe. These are in accordance with the working of the strength of His might which He brought about in Christ, when He raised Him from the dead, and seated Him at His right hand in the heavenly places, far above all rule and authority and power and dominion, and every name that is named, not only in this age, but also in the one to come. And He put all things in subjection under His feet, and gave Him as head over all things to the church, which is His body, the fulness of Him who fills all in all."[18]

As we walk through life and face various spiritual battles, we need to assume our rightful position in Christ. Above all we must take up the shield of faith with which we will be able to extinguish *all* the fiery darts of the evil one.

8

Life's "75%"

There are seasons of life when we can feel very discouraged because of all the trials and struggles we are experiencing. A friend of mine, Don Meredith, founder of Christian Family Life, a family counseling and teaching ministry, has an interesting theory about such times.

Recently his secretary, Carol Wierman, was pouring out her heart to him concerning the many difficult circumstances she was facing. When she finished, Don said, "Carol, what you have just told me is not unusual. Seventy-five percent of life is made up of struggles, concerns, frustrations and trials. That 75% will always be with you. Now what you need to do is let your life be characterized in that 75%, not with unbelief, but with faith, by believing God and hoping in Him."

Then he added whimsically, "In the other 25%, trust the Lord and go out and have a good time."

When Carol related the incident to me, I thought Don's counsel contained great wisdom. Jesus Himself had taught that in this world we would have troubles. Yet we are often deceived into thinking we really shouldn't have problems and that "happiness is just around the corner."

We get caught up in the "when-then" syndrome. "When I'm out of school, *then* everything will be o.k." "When I get married, *then* I'll be happy." "When I get out of this hard spot, *then* everything will be fine." And on it goes.

But that's not what usually happens.

As Don suggested, it is not uncommon for us to go through difficulties and heartaches. We feel the pain, but we may not know how to be objective about the experience. Understandably, it is often hard to isolate those incidents, to stand back from them and evaluate what is going on. As a result, we may never benefit from the experience.

I have learned that a very real part of walking by faith every day is being able to "objectify" life's experiences. There is a simple chart I like to use in helping me to objectify my own "75%."

The first thing I do, as I begin thinking through a given circumstance, is to divide a piece of paper into four parts or columns.

In the first column, I record *every good and positive thing* I can think of about the situation. For example, if my struggles center around a certain person, I write down everything I like about that individual.

In the second column, I try to think of and list all the negative aspects about the matter; I include anything I *dislike.* Usually these are things that are hard for me to accept.

Someone has said that negative circumstances and people do not put negative reactions in our hearts, they merely reveal what is already there. The old adage, "He brings out the worst in me" holds a good deal of truth; "he" didn't *put in* "the worst," but he did bring it out! Often I'm not aware of the "negatives" in my heart until something comes into my life to expose them.

In column three I write down *my responses* to the things I mentioned in column two. I have found it essential to be very honest about my inner reactions and responses. This column always brings to light a variety of attitudes such as hate, irritability, lack of forgiveness or impatience.

My next step in this column is to confess to the Lord the things I have written down. Often the attitudes that come out are just the opposite of the fruit of the Spirit—love, joy, peace, patience, kindness, gentleness, goodness.[1] I say, "Lord, I agree with You that I am wrong and You are right."

In column four I write down *what God seems to be wanting to teach me* through my situation. For instance, if I find hate in my heart, then God might be wanting to teach me how to love. If I find impatience, perhaps He is wanting to teach me patience.

Then I pull out a good Bible concordance or a helpful guide such as *Nave's Topical Bible* to find appropriate verses to meet my need.

Here is a sample chart:

Things I like	Things I don't like
My reactions or My responses	What God might want to teach me or Scripture to meet my need

After I have put all my thoughts and feelings on paper, I like to go back and thank God for everything I've written in columns two and three. I do this knowing that He will work even these things together for good in my life.

When I see my responses in the third column, although I see how far short they fall from Scripture, I have learned not to get down on myself or become discouraged. Although I may grieve over the sin in my heart that is revealed, I do not condemn myself, because God doesn't condemn me.

Rather I am free to admit my sinfulness, knowing that to be truthful with the Lord about what is in my heart is the first step toward change.

I have been encouraged by the little booklet, *The Practice of the Presence of God*, by Brother Lawrence, a 17th century Christian.

Brother Lawrence walked very closely with the Lord. When he sinned, he would lift up his hand toward heaven and say to God, "I shall never do otherwise if You leave me to myself."[2] He cast himself on the Lord, realizing that he needed the Lord's power in order to live the Christian life.

I have often quoted Brother Lawrence's words to the Lord, and in addition have prayed, "Father, do for me by Your Holy Spirit what I cannot do for myself."

I used to look at Scripture as a "law" or a "threat" being held over my head, condemning me for not living up to its standards. Now I see that God's Word is not meant to be a threat, but a promise of all that He wants to do in my life by His Spirit.

Through the years people have said to me, "Ney, I have confessed a particular sin over and over, but I haven't seen any progress." They will usually be naming a specific action or attitude that might be found in column three of the chart.

My question to them has often been, "Are you renewing your mind with a portion of Scripture that speaks to what you have confessed?" More often than not, they will say they had not thought of doing that. In other words, they may have confessed "impatience," but they have not gone on to think or meditate on a passage of Scripture that deals with "patience," in order to gain God's perspective.

Since God convicts us of *specific* sin in our lives, such as impatience, we need to confess those sins specifically. Then we need to fill our minds with a portion of God's Word that relates *specifically* to what we've confessed. In this way, the Holy Spirit can take that portion of Scripture and begin t renew our minds with God's perspective.

One of the benefits of using the chart is that even though the second column focuses on what we don't like about a person or a situation, we end in column four by taking personal responsibility for our own behavior and finding a passage of Scripture that will minister to our need. The person or circumstance that initially seemed to be like a millstone around our necks becomes a blessing God has given to teach us more about His character.

One of those circumstances came into my life in January of 1977.

It all began when Robert Pittenger, an assistant to Dr. Bright, greeted me as he arrived at our home for dinner. "Ney, I've been thinking that you should go to the presidential inauguration in Washington, D.C. Carol Lawrence (well-known singer and actress) has been asked by Jimmy Carter to sing, and since we will be hosting her time there it would be nice if you could go and be with her. I'm going to telex Dr. Bright in Africa and see if he thinks it would be a good idea."

The whole matter seemed fantastic but far-fetched to me.

"I really do appreciate your wanting me to go, Robert, but I don't know . . . God would have to do a lot to work out all the details on such short notice. I leave on a trip in a couple of days, so I'll just assume I'm not going unless I hear from you."

Two days later I flew to Seattle to speak at a Campus Crusade staff conference, then on to Little Rock, Arkansas, for another conference. I arrived in Little Rock in the late afternoon and checked into my hotel. There was a message awaiting me at the front desk, asking me to call Dr. Bright's office at Arrowhead Springs.

I dialed the number, and Jim Pratt, also an assistant to Dr. Bright, answered. "Ney, Dr. Bright definitely wants you to go the inauguration."

"He really does, Jim?"

"Yes, it's all set. They're expecting you."

I hung up the phone in a daze. I exclaimed aloud, "Is this really happening to me? Lord, what will I wear?" I had nothing that would be suitable for such a formal occasion, nor did I have enough money to buy anything.

During my introductory remarks that night at the conference, I shared my news. Normally I would stay for the whole conference, but this time I would be leaving to go to Dallas and then on to the inauguration. The conferees were excited for me.

Returning to my hotel room that evening after the meeting, my overwhelming thoughts were of concern and worry over what I would wear in Washington, D.C. I propped up in bed, pillows at my back, and picked up my Bible. I was so accustomed by now to using the "objectifying" chart, it had become second nature to me. I mentally started through the steps and began to analyze the situation carefully.

I *liked* the thought of going to Washington. I *didn't like* it that I didn't have the right clothes to wear or the money to buy them. My *reaction* was to become anxious. I hadn't been aware of some of the worry and unbelief in my heart until this incident revealed it. I confessed my anxiety, realizing that the Lord was wanting to *teach* me faith.

Then I remembered a place in the Sermon on the Mount in which Jesus was speaking to those who were anxious about food and clothing. I quickly turned there and began to read,

"For this reason I say to you, do not be anxious
for your life, as to what you shall eat, or what you

shall drink; nor for your body, as to what you shall put on . . . . Observe how the lilies of the field grow; they do not toil nor do they spin, yet I say to you that even Solomon in all his glory did not clothe himself like one of these. But if God so arrays the grass of the field, which is alive today and tomorrow is thrown into the furnace, will He not much more do so for you, O men [women] of little faith?"[3]

"Lord, I confess to You that I'm anxious about 'what I shall put on.' But You say here that You clothe the lilies and the grass and that You'll do *much more* for me. I do confess my 'little faith!' I want to believe You!"

"Do not be anxious then, saying 'What shall we eat?' or 'What shall we drink?' or, 'With what shall we clothe ourselves?' For all these things the Gentiles eagerly seek; for your heavenly Father knows that you need all these things. But seek first His kingdom and His righteousness; and all these things shall be added to you."[4]

"Oh, Lord, as best I know how, I am seeking first Your kingdom and Your righteousness. But I'm so glad You know my needs, that You will take care of me; that all these things 'will be added' to me. I believe Your Word is truer than how I feel right now, and I pray that You will provide—and I thank You for how that will be done."

I turned off the lights and slipped under the covers. I lay there drifting into sleep singing the little song, "Seek and ye shall find, knock and the door shall be opened . . . . " It occurred to me I could start "seeking" and "knocking" by looking for some clothes I could borrow.

The next morning I realized I needed to cash a small check to cover the rest of my trip. My friend, Carol Wierman, was registrar for the conference and offered to cash the check for me.

She brought me the money while I was sitting in the back of a room during a meeting. Kneeling by my chair, she handed me two extra $10 bills and whispered, "Ney, I'd like this to go toward something for your trip."

I handed the extra money back to her. "Carol," I protested. "you're dear to do this, but I can't take it!"

She handed the bills back insistently. "Ney, I want you to have it. I believe the Lord wants me to give it to you." Carol walked away, leaving me with a lump in my throat and two $10 bills in my lap.

Later in the day another friend at the conference, Ann Parkinson, handed me a note. My mouth fell open in amazement when I unfolded it and out fell $30.

I was still holding the note in my hand when Don Meredith, the conference speaker, came up to me and said, "Well, have you been shopping yet for the inauguration?"

"No, Don, I really wasn't planning on shopping. I thought I'd borrow something to wear."

He was indignant. "I don't want you to borrow anything. I want you to buy yourself a new outfit. Can Christian Family Life give you $150?" Before I could answer, he had his checkbook out, writing out that amount. I was speechless!

Late that night I sat in my hotel room, my chin resting in my hands, staring at three $10 bills, one $20 bill and a check for $150. I worshipped the Lord as I viewed the display of money which had come in direct response to my need, less than 24 hours after my prayer. I was overwhelmed with joy.

I called a friend long distance to share with her my elation over what the Lord had done. After I related the story she said, "I'd like to add $25 to what the Lord has already given."

And there was still more to come.

I left Little Rock on Sunday and decided to stop in Dallas. My roommate, Mary Graham, and I had been invited to a church building dedication set for that evening.

I met Mary at the airport, and as we arrived at the church, we were spotted by a friend of mine, Ann West, who rushed up to us.

"Ney, what are you doing in Dallas?"

"Annie, you won't believe this, but I'm on my way to the inauguration."

"Really? That's great! What are you going to wear?"

"Funny you should ask. I plan to shop for something tomorrow. And Ann Parkinson suggested I should call a friend of hers to borrow a couple of long dresses."

"You don't need to do that! I have some things I know you could wear. Come on over tonight."

Midnight found me going through Ann's closet, trying on black velvet skirts and lovely gowns. When Mary and I left the West's home a little later, I had two elegant gowns that would be suitable for any evening event in Washington.

The next day, with the money from the Little Rock conference I bought a beautiful five-piece suit with skirt and slacks at an exclusive Dallas department store.

The woman doing my alterations was hemming the slacks when I remarked, "You know, this is the most expensive outfit I've ever bought."

"Ya gotta be kiddin'!" she said in a strong Eastern accent, looking up in surprise.

"No, it really is."

"Well, what'sa deal?" she asked. "Where are ya goin'?"

"Do you really want to know?"

"Yeah, tell me."

I reviewed for her my invitation to the inauguration and how, not having anything to wear, God provided for my needs miraculously. With reverence in her voice she said, "I've been head of this department for seven years; I've never done this before and I will never do it again, but because you've told me this story, I'm not going to charge you anything for the alteration." Not only did she alter free of charge, but she completed in two hours what often takes several days.

That night as I was packing to leave for Washington, I surveyed my clothing: two lovely gowns, the suit, a new purse, new shoes, some new costume jewelry. The Lord had done "exceeding abundantly"[5] beyond all that I could have asked or thought.

The next morning Mary bade me goodbye at the Dallas airport. As I waited to board my plane, I felt a little anxious about the new and different situations I would be facing over the next few days. I pulled out my Bible and turned to Matthew 6. The chapter's last verse stood out:

> "Therefore, do not be anxious for tomorrow; for tomorrow will care for itself. Each day has enough trouble of its own."[6]

I silently prayed, "Lord, I thank You again for Your miraculous provision for me. Thank You for the opportunity to go to Washington. Now I choose to believe that tomorrow will care for itself . . . that *You* will take care of me . . . I don't have grace yet for my tomorrows, but I thank You that Your grace will be sufficient when tomorrow comes."

The announcement came to board the plane. Seated next to me on the plane was a distinguished couple who also happened to be going to the inauguration. The husband was a man of many titles, including being the former head of the Bureau of Indian Affairs. By the time we landed, I had been invited to be the couple's guest at the American Indian Inaugural Ball!

Robert Pittenger, who had first mentioned to me the possibility of attending the inauguration, was at the Washington National Airport to meet my plane.

"Ney, Carol Lawrence's agent just called to say she is ill and won't be able to come."

"That's o.k., Robert. The Lord has already outdone Himself for me on this trip. I know I'm here for a purpose."

The Lord's blessing on my trip was evident in countless ways. I made many new friends, visited the White House and Executive Office Building, attended the American Indian Ball and observed the nation's capital in festive transition.

And I had some important spiritual lessons reinforced during those days of exciting preparation. I believe the turnabout in my attitudes concerning the inauguration came when I recognized my anxiety and made it a point to get into a portion of Scripture that would speak to my need.

I was anxious and needed clothes. I could have stopped there and worried—which I have done in the past. But because I had learned to objectify my circumstances, I was able to gain God's perspective on the situation.

In reading Matthew 6, I was able to renew my mind with God's words and see my situation from His perspective. I was honest with Him about my feelings, but I chose to believe Scripture. I claimed His promises that He would meet my need, long before I *felt* like my need would be met.

Our crisis points come in varying degrees, from small difficulties to major conflicts. Whether we're faced with the normal "ups and downs" of life or the hardest things we've ever encountered, we need to remember that our "75%" will continue to be with us the rest of our lives. But these circumstances can turn out to be God's greatest supernatural blessings for us—if we learn to objectify our experiences and trust Him in the midst of them.

9

Failure and the Phantom

There have been times when my relationship with the Lord has been so close and satisfying that I've thought, "For the rest of my life, all I will do is just love and serve and please Him. I'm finally getting the picture of the Christian life, finally walking in victory. From now on, everything will be just fine."

But just about the time I think I've got it all together and think I'll never fail again, I surprise myself. I fail.

I guess because I'm surprised, my tendency is to assume God is surprised too.

I remember one time failing in a way I thought I would never fail again. Terribly depressed and despondent, I wondered how someone as sinful as I ever wound up in Christian work.

Jean and I were living together at the time, and she noticed my "slough of despond."

She said sympathetically, "Ney, God is not surprised that you failed."

Hardly believing her words, I exclaimed, "He's not?"

As if to reinforce the truth to my heart, Jean repeated, "No, God is not surprised that you failed."

"But Jean, sometimes I wish I could just be perfect. I don't want to sin, but I always fall short of my standard of perfection. I am very discouraged over my failure."

"I understand how you feel, Ney. You know, it's interesting, but at the point in time when we accept Christ, we know that we are totally loved and forgiven. But as we grow in the Christian life, something happens.

"Maybe we begin comparing ourselves with other people who seem more spiritually mature; or we look at the standards of an organization of which we are a part; or we look at the standards of Scripture. When we fall short of any of those standards, we start condemning ourselves.

"When that happens, we have forgotten that God is the one who causes the growth and gives the increase.[1]

"No matter where we are right now in our growth, we are right on schedule. We are still totally loved and accepted by Him. God is not surprised that we are where we are."

I listened with great interest as she continued.

"What can happen is a great gap forms between where we are and where we want to be; between the 'phantom' image in our minds of where we think we should be spiritually and where we are in reality. So we start trying to bridge the gap in our own strength.

"Then we start trying to perform in the flesh, to achieve our growth by self-effort, forgetting that as we seek the Lord and His ways, His Spirit is the One who causes the growth in us."

My tendency was to think that God accepted me when I was being obedient and all was going well in my Christian life. But I couldn't see how God could love and accept me when I stumbled and failed; when I was falling flat on my face spiritually and life was looking dark and difficult because of my mistakes.

As Jean talked, I began to sense relief from internal pressure for the first time in several days. She was making a lot of sense just by giving me God's perspective. I was beginning to see that even though I had failed, He hadn't given up on me.

I was reminded that God loved and accepted me regardless of my performance—a reminder which encouraged me beyond measure to want my life to come in line with His Word in every way. And though the meaning of forgiveness is *to cancel a debt as if it never happened*, realizing this did not make me think I was being given a license to sin willfully and go my own way. Instead, I was motivated more to want to please Him in every area of my life.

I realized that I could not look inside myself and find peace or justification while looking at my merits or performance. But I could look at what God said about me, my forgiveness and my position and acceptance in Christ, choose with my will to believe it and find peace.

Paul wrote, "Therefore having been justified by faith, we have peace with God through our Lord Jesus Christ."[2] My *position* in Christ remained unchanging; it was my daily *condition, or behavior and performance*, that was so variable and changing.

Those of us who have put our faith in Christ are not on probation. God knows that we are not Christians who became human beings at a point in time; rather, we are human beings who became Christians at a point in time. Even before He showered His love, mercy and grace on us He knew our weaknesses and frailties.

Since Christ died for me while I was a helpless, ungodly, sinful enemy, it became clear to me that there was nothing I could do to improve my image and make Him love me more. He loved me as much then as He ever would and as much as He ever has.[3]

Jesus said, "Just as the Father has loved Me, I have also loved you."[4] Just as God will not take His love back from Jesus, neither will God take His love back from me. He made an eternal covenant with me that will never be broken.

How did I know that God would be understanding, merciful and forgiving toward me and my failures? One way was through the example of Jesus.

Christ's earthly ministry was characterized by forgiveness and compassion: as He freed the adulteress from her sin in the presence of those ready to stone her; as He was accused of blasphemy by religious leaders for claiming to have the authority to forgive sins; even as He hung on the cross and gave eternal life to the criminal being crucified with Him. Jesus said, "He who has seen Me has seen the Father."[5] Jesus demonstrated visibly the forgiveness of God.

Among the numerous instances in which Jesus forgave people, one of the most personally encouraging examples is how the Lord treated Peter after he failed.

Simon Peter was one of the first disciples chosen by the Lord. There are many scenes which show Peter in his spontaneity and wholeheartedness. He was giving, thoughtful, loyal and protective of Christ. He demonstrated great faith, spoke the truth from his heart and said what he thought. Peter was one of Christ's closest friends while He was on the earth, and he loved Him with abandon.

But perhaps Peter's devotion to Christ was never more fully evident than at the Last Supper. As Jesus gathered His disciples around Him to tell them what the next hours and days would hold, He turned His attention to Peter.

> " 'Simon, Simon, behold, Satan has demanded permission to sift you like wheat; but I have prayed for you, that your faith may not fail; and you, when once you have turned again, strengthen your brothers.' And he said to Him, 'Lord, with You I am ready to go both to prison and to death!' And He said, 'I tell you, Peter, the cock will not crow today until you have denied three times that you know Me.' Peter said to Him, 'Even if I must die with You, I will not deny You.' "[6]

Peter couldn't imagine ever forsaking the Lord, and even when Christ told him of the imminent denial, Peter refused to believe he could ever do such a thing.

And then came the moment which Peter could not conceive of ever happening. The hours following the Last Supper had been traumatic and painful. Peter had gone with Christ to the Garden of Gethsemane, where he witnessed Judas' betrayal.

It was there also that Peter, in anguish over the betrayal and Christ's abusive arrest by Roman officials, impulsively drew a sword and cut off the ear of the high priest's slave.

Luke records the events following Jesus' arrest:

> "And having arrested Him they led Him away, and brought Him to the house of the high priest; *but Peter was following at a distance.* And after they had kindled a fire in the middle of the courtyard and had sat down together, Peter was sitting among them. And a certain servant-girl, seeing him as he sat in the firelight, and looking intently at him, said 'This man was with Him too.' But he denied it, saying, 'Woman, I do not know Him.' And a little later, another saw him and said, 'You are one of them too!' But Peter said, 'Man, I am not!' And after about an hour had passed, another man began to insist, saying, 'Certainly this man also was with Him, for he is a Galilean too.' But Peter said, 'Man, I do not know what you are talking about.' And immediately, while he was still speaking, a cock crowed. And the Lord *turned and looked* at Peter. And Peter *remembered the word* of the Lord, how He had told him, 'Before a cock crows today, you will deny Me three times.' And he went outside and *wept bitterly*"[7] [italics mine].

Jesus was not surprised when Peter failed. He had even prayed for Peter earlier that the disciple's faith would not fail. Notice that Jesus' prayer wasn't for *Peter* not to fail, but that Peter's *faith* wouldn't fail.

I believe Christ was saying that when Peter failed, he needed to believe that he was *still loved* and that he was *forgiven.* In essence, Jesus was telling him, "In spite of what happens, Peter, I want you to believe what I have told you; I want you to take Me at My word that I love you . . . that you have forgiveness."

Further evidence of Christ's forgiveness came on resurrection

morning. Mary Magdalene and two other grieving followers of
the Lord had just discovered the empty tomb. Empty, that is,
except for an angel sitting in the tomb, waiting to give them
the message that the Savior was risen.

I've always loved what the angel said:

> " . . . He has risen; He is not here; behold, here is
> the place where they laid Him. *But go, tell His disciples
> and Peter*"[8] [italics mine].

It seems that here the Lord shows a special concern for
Peter's state of mind. When Peter heard the news of the resurrection, he literally ran to the tomb to see for himself that Jesus
had risen.

Christ made a number of post-resurrection appearances
during the 40-day period before His ascension. One of those
appearances sheds even more light on the Lord's forgiveness of
Peter.

One day Peter and the other disciples went fishing on the
Sea of Galilee and had little success. They fished on through the
night and caught nothing.

As the next day was breaking, Jesus appeared on the beach
and called out to them, "Children, you do not have any fish,
do you?"

The disciples, who had not yet recognized who He was,
answered, "No." Then Jesus instructed them, "Cast the net on
the right-hand side of the boat, and you will find a catch."

The disciples cast the net, and so many fish were caught
that the men, several of whom were fishermen by trade, couldn't
haul in the net. When this happened, John said to Peter, "It is
the Lord." And when Peter heard those words, he threw himself
into the sea, swimming as fast as he could to reach Jesus on
shore.

If Peter hadn't known he was forgiven for his failure and
that he was still loved by the Lord, would he have jumped from
the boat out of eagerness to see Jesus?

More than likely, he would have covered himself with the nets and hidden in the bottom of the boat. Then when the disciples came to shore and Jesus asked, "Where's Peter?" they would have answered, "Lord, he is afraid of You. He doesn't want to see You because he knows how angry You'll be with him for what he did."

But Peter was so convinced of Jesus' love and forgiveness that as soon as he discovered it was Jesus on the shore, he swam the length of a football field to meet Him.

Peter was with the Lord day and night for at least three years. He had heard Christ teach on forgiveness; he had seen Him forgive others. He may have even heard Christ cry out on the cross in behalf of those who crucified Him, "Father, forgive them; for they do not know what they are doing."[9]

Now Peter had the opportunity to accept Christ's forgiveness for himself. Jesus had prayed that Peter's faith would not fail. And in the midst of the tragic crucifixion night, this heartbroken disciple managed to remember the Lord's words and turned back to Him, believing that he was still loved and forgiven in spite of everything.

Peter must have also learned of the *totality* of Christ's love, a love that "does not take into account a wrong suffered."[10] Jesus didn't throw Peter's failure in his face. In fact, the Bible does not record Christ ever mentioning the denials after the Last Supper—a wonderful fulfillment of God's promise that He will remove our sins as far as the east is from the west[11] and will "remember [our sins] no more."[12]

In vivid contrast, Satan loves to make the most of our failures. For through them, he can fully assume his role as "the accuser of the brethren," causing us to think, "I'm totally inadequate . . . I'm just not 'spiritual' enough . . . I don't know enough . . . I'm not doing enough for God . . . "

But it is the Lord Jesus Christ who justifies and accepts us and can even use those failures for His glory. In *Principles of Spiritual Growth*, J.C. Metcalfe is quoted as saying, "Without a bitter experience of our own inadequacy and poverty [we] are quite unfitted to bear the burden of spiritual ministry. It takes a man who has discovered something of the measures of his own weakness to be patient with the foibles of others.

"Such a man also has a first-hand knowledge of the loving care of the Chief Shepherd, and His ability to heal one who has come humbly to trust in Him and Him alone. Therefore he does not easily despair of others, but looks beyond sinfulness, willfulness and stupidity, to the might of unchanging love.

"The Lord Jesus does not give the charge, 'Be a shepherd to my lambs . . . to My sheep,' on hearing Peter's self-confident affirmation of undying loyalty, but He gives it after he has utterly failed to keep his vows and has wept bitterly in the streets of Jerusalem."[13]

I have often put myself in Peter's place, and I can relate closely to all that he went through—how he saw the Lord from a distance, failed Him and wondered how God could possibly love him and use him again. In the same way, during the incident I mentioned earlier when I felt I had failed Him so greatly, I wondered if God still loved me and would ever use me again.

But as I meditated on God's perfect love for me, His love cast out any fear in my heart.[14] I came to see that God loves me as I am, just as He loved Peter. And He forgave me, just as He forgave Peter. The Lord looked beyond my failures and inconsistencies into my heart attitude of repentance and my sincere desire to please Him.

Wherever we are right now, we are loved and forgiven. We are "right on schedule" according to God's timetable. He who has begun a good work in us will continue to perform it.[15] God will not forsake the work of His own hands.[16]

Just as Peter knew when he recognized Christ on the seashore, it is never too late to "swim" to Him.

It is never too late to begin again.

10

How Firm a Foundation?

I had been invited to speak at a student conference in Washington, D. C. Following the conference, a good friend, Winky Leinster, and I decided to take a Sunday drive across the Virginia countryside. Winky started out as the driver, and after one of the stops I offered to drive.

The lovely green rolling hills, with quaint farmhouses tucked back in groves of trees, made the outing thoroughly enjoyable. We were basking in the beauty of our surroundings as we came over a hill, only to see several police cars on the grassy middle-ground of the freeway.

"Uh-oh, Wink. I think this is a speed trap. I'm going over 60, and this is a 55 speed zone. I think I'm in trouble."

One of the police cars pulled out immediately as we passed, with its red light flashing.

I pulled off the road onto the shoulder. My heart was pounding.

A nice-looking, dark-haired highway patrolman approached Winky's car—a light green Chevrolet that she affectionately called "Sweet Pea." I rolled down my window.

The officer's manner was matter-of-fact, and his face expressionless as he asked, "May I see your driver's license?"

I handed it to him through the window. He looked it over intently.

"You wear contacts?"

"Yes."

He looked closely at my eyes to verify my statement. "You're from out of state?"

"Yes, I live in California. I'm just here on a brief visit."

"Did you know you were going 70 miles an hour in a 55 speed zone?"

"I know I was going over 60, but I don't think I was going 70."

"We clocked you at 70 miles an hour, and you'll have to come with me into the next town to see the magistrate. Since you're from out of town, you'll have to face charges today."

"The magistrate? Officer, we're on our way back to D.C. where I need to catch a plane in the morning. Can't I settle this with you? I really don't have time to spare."

"I'm sorry, but you will have to follow me into town to see the magistrate."

By this time I was groping for a way to get off the hook. "My dad's a lawyer. Isn't there some way I could take care of this with you and settle it by mail?"

Totally unmoved by my parentage or my pleas, the officer said, "No, I'm sorry, you'll have to come with me to see the magistrate."

"How long do you think this will take?"

"It depends on how long it takes us to locate her and how busy she is. Now, if you'll just follow me into town . . . "

He started walking back to his car. I took a deep breath and restarted the engine.

"Well, he was all business, wasn't he?" Winky said supportively. "Nothing seemed to matter to him. All he was concerned about was that the law was broken and that you needed to go before the judge."

As we followed the patrolman mile after mile into town, it was beginning to seem like a bad dream.

"Wink, I can't believe this is happening."

"Neither can I."

"This is unreal, getting taken into a 'magistrate'! I've never heard anyone use that title before. Usually they say 'judge.'"

"Let's pray." We thanked the Lord for our predicament and asked God for grace and favor in the eyes of the magistrate.

We came into the business district of Culpeper, passing hamburger stands, service stations, and then on into the older part of town.

As we rounded a corner, there stood a quaint old two-story courthouse that appeared to come out of another era. Surrounding the building was an equally old wrought iron fence with a sign on it that loomed large: JAIL IN REAR.

The officer preceded us through the gate and headed around the building toward the back.

"Wink, do you see that? Jail! We're headed for the jail! I can't believe this."

As we disembarked from Winky's car, we tromped over a cobblestone path and through a dilapidated door to face immediately a large, long white counter. Behind it our arresting officer was telephoning the magistrate.

We stood in front of the counter, taking in the setting. Close by on our left were iron bars and cells. Through the opening we could hear prisoners talking.

The wall behind us was covered with—of all things—"Wanted" posters. The gray, solemn faces staring out at us, complete with numbers and statistics, added to the jail atmosphere.

"Miss Bailey, I need to ask you some questions."

I turned toward the counter to see the officer with some forms on a clipboard. He went through the questions and came to the one titled, "Employer."

A bit embarrassed, I said, "Believe it or not, I work with Campus Crusade for Christ International."

This was the first time I had seen even a glimmer of a smile in his eyes. But he made no reply.

After the questions, I said, "I see you have a coffee maker just like mine. Makes great coffee." My comment seemed to break the ice further and soften his business-like manner. Warmly he offered, "Would you like a cup?"

"Yes, I'd love one. Thank you."

He gave me the coffee and continued standing at the counter facing the front door, recording something on his clipboard. His writing was interrupted when the door flew open, and a large, gray-haired woman came barreling through like a cyclone. She stepped over the threshold and continued in motion toward her inner office. Without so much as a glance in the officer's direction, she blurted out in rapid-fire succession the words,

"Do-you-swear-to-tell-the-whole-truth-and-nothing-but-the-truth-so-help-you-God?"

The officer was just responding with his customary "I do" as she landed in her office. Winky wondered if he didn't feel a little foolish with his right hand stuck up in the air while the judge was already two rooms away.

I whispered to Winky, "Try not to laugh" as we attempted to contain our amusement at what seemed like a scene from a situation comedy on television.

We had been waiting about 10 minutes when the officer, who had remained with us, said, "You can go in now."

As we walked into the magistrate's office, she did not look up or say a word or acknowledge us in any way. I wondered if the officer hadn't sent us in prematurely. Winky and I exchanged quizzical glances. I almost felt invisible as we stood shifting from one foot to the other for 10 more minutes while the judge busied herself with papers on her desk.

Then without looking up, she said authoritatively, "You were going 70 miles an hour in a 55 mile zone. That will be $50 or a day in jail."

I had figured my finances while we were waiting in the lobby, and responding with some relief, I said, "Well, amazingly enough, that's just about what I have in my checking account."

She looked up abruptly as I reached for my purse and spoke with a tone of disgust. "We can't take your check!"

"You can't?" I said with astonishment. "It would be perfectly good, and I have all kinds of identification."

"That doesn't matter. We don't take out-of-state checks.

You'll have to spend the night in jail!"

Winky and I looked at each other in dismay.

"I'm a Virginia resident," Winky offered. "My parents live in Vienna, Virginia. Can you take my check?"

"No. What about your parents? Could they send money?"

"I'm sure they would if they could, but they are enroute to South Carolina. There is no possible way I could reach them before tomorrow."

The magistrate looked back at me and said firmly, "You'll have to spend the night in jail."

I knew I had no choice. I had broken the law. It didn't matter to the judge who I was, or what my occupation was, or the fact that my father was a lawyer. My identification and checks were unacceptable. I couldn't pay the penalty.

I would have to go to jail. That was all there was to it.

I thought, "This will be a first! Wait until my friends hear about this!"

The policeman, who had entered the room a few minutes earlier, stepped forward and said to Winky, "If you want to write me a personal check for $50, I'll cash it for you out of my pocket. And then you'll have the money to pay the fine."

Motioning toward the magistrate, I said, "Why can you cash a check and she can't?"

"Because I'm offering to do this personally and not as a part of the court."

Before he had a chance to change his mind, Winky took him up on his offer. She wrote out a check for $50, and he handed her $50 in cash. Then Winky, in turn, gave the $50 to the magistrate and paid my penalty for me. A receipt was given for the charges marked, "Paid in full."

At last, I was free to go!

The officer walked out the door with us. His parting words were, "Ladies, try not to speed from now on."

I felt like I had been "through the wringer." When we reached our car, I smiled and said, "I've driven enough for one day. You drive."

As we pulled away from the Culpeper courthouse, we prayed once again, thanking the Lord for all we had been through. We asked Him to teach us from the experience.

As we began to discuss what had just happened, it dawned on us what a perfect illustration it made for what Christ had done on the cross.

I had broken the law by speeding and was sentenced to pay the penalty of $50 or a day in jail. Since I couldn't pay the penalty, Winky paid it for me. All I had to do was accept what she had done for me—which I gladly did.

In like manner, we have all broken God's laws and must pay the penalty, which is death. But God sent Christ to die for our sins, to pay the penalty for us as a gift. All we need to do is accept Him and what He's done for us on the cross.

As we discussed the analogy, Winky said, "Ney, I would like to do what I've done for you as a gift."

"You're kidding," I said. "You don't mean it . . . you want to pay *my* fine?"

"Yes, I really want to. And besides, if you paid me back, our analogy would break down!"

It was near dusk as we drove back toward Washington, D.C. "I will never forget this day," I thought. "And I'll never forget Culpeper, Virginia!"

If everyone could catch as clear a picture of what Christ has done for us as Winky and I did through our experience in Virginia, it would seem natural that everyone would want to allow Christ to come into his life.

But I find that many people are confused as to what it actually means to become a Christian, to be "born again." I recently heard about a woman who said to her friend, "I'm not born again yet, but I keep trying and trying!" She did not realize that becoming a Christian is so simple a child can understand the process—it's a matter of believing in Jesus Christ and saying "yes" to Him.

God often has people cross my path who are not yet Christians but who are spiritually hungry and want to know God.

This kind of experience has happened to me more times than I can count. One of the most memorable was the night of the Big Thompson flood.

During our harrowing escape up the dark, slippery mountain, the night of the disastrous onslaught of flood waters, someone in our group paused to help an older woman on the steep incline. When the police signaled us to return to the road below, she was the first person I saw. I gave her a big hug and exclaimed, "I'm so glad you're o.k.!"

"Who are you—and why are you being so good to me?" she asked.

Without hesitation I said, "I would hope that if my mother were ever caught in something like this, someone would be there to help—"

Before I could finish my sentence the urgent voices of police ordered us to get in our cars immediately and line up caravan-style to wait for further instructions. It was very cold and raining hard as I raced 50 yards to the car I had thought I would never see again. I was relieved that it started with ease —it hadn't always!

When I returned to the point where the caravan was forming, the lady, her husband and Jackie Hudson got in my car to wait.

They had been in the car only a few seconds when her husband said, "I'm going to see if I can find our trailer up ahead. I've got some whiskey in there, and I need it."

As he shut the door, the woman said again, "Who are you and why are you being so good to us?"

"We are staff members with Campus Crusade for Christ, an interdenominational Christian organization," I answered. "We came here today for a retreat and were staying just across the river at the Sylvan Dale Ranch when we heard the warnings to evacuate. Some of our women are still on the other side, and we're concerned about them."

"I've heard of Campus Crusade. I've been a church member for years."

"May I ask you a question? In all these years of being a church member have you ever made the discovery of knowing Christ personally for yourself?"

She shook her head. "I've been in church all my life, but I don't think I know Him like you're talking about."

"I don't know how much time we have, but let me tell you how you can know Him."

It was dark, the windows were foggy, and we could barely see each other's faces as I began.

"The first thing is that God loves you. John 3:16 says, 'For God so loved the world, that He gave His only begotten Son, that whoever believes in Him should not perish, but have eternal life.' You can replace 'world' with your own name. By the way," I smiled, "what is your name?"

"Lou."

"Then the verse would read, 'For God so loved Lou, that He gave His only begotten Son, that if Lou believes in Him she should not perish, but have eternal life.'"

"It's like this, Lou." In the condensation on the windshield I drew two parallel lines, one across the top and one at the lower portion. "God is up here, 'way above us, and He is holy. Men and women are down here, and we are sinful."

I drew some arrows from the lower portion reaching about halfway up the windshield. "We try to reach up to God in a number of ways, but the Bible says we all have sinned and have fallen short of the glory of God.[1] Basically that means that none of us is as good as God is, and we are prone to go our own way with little or no thought of God.

"And the Bible says we earn something for our sin. 'For the wages of sin is death, but the gift of God is eternal life through Jesus Christ our Lord.'"[2]

Her eyes were glued on me as she listened intently.

"Sin was a word that quite frankly used to bother me. I didn't like it at all. Then someone told me to imagine putting everything I've ever done in my life on film, projecting the movie on a large screen and then inviting all my neighbors and friends to come see it. Now if you are like me, there would be some things you wouldn't want them to see!"

"Oh, yes," she exclaimed. "There are things that I wouldn't want to be up there."

"Well," I replied, "those are the things that the Bible calls sin. Those are the things Jesus died for." Then I superimposed the cross of Christ between the parallel lines, illustrating how Jesus had paid the penalty for our sin, our separation, bridging the gap between God and man. "When I first saw that, Lou—that Jesus bridges the gap—I finally understood where Jesus fit into the picture. It had never made sense to me before.

"Jesus is God's only provision for our sin and through Him we can know God's love and plan for our lives. You've probably heard that He said, 'I am the way, and the truth, and the life; no one comes to the Father, but through Me.'"[3]

"Yes, I've heard that."

"It's not enough to know these things. We may have grown up hearing them. You know, many people will tell us we ought to become Christians, but very few people ever tell us how. And this is the last, and most important point—the how-to. We must individually receive Jesus Christ as Savior and Lord by personal invitation. That means that no one else can receive Him for us.

"Jesus said, 'Behold, I stand at the door and knock'—that is the door of your heart and life—'if anyone hears My voice and opens the door'—and we either will or we won't . . . it is a matter of our wills—Christ says, 'I will come in.'[4]

"Lou, do you think you'd like to ask Him into your life?"

"Oh, yes, and I'd like to do that right now."

"We receive Christ by faith, Lou, and our faith can be expressed through prayer. Why don't you pray, asking Christ to come into your life, and then Jackie and I will pray for you."

She began, "Lord Jesus, I need You. I thank You for dying for me and all those things that would be up on the screen of my life. I ask You to come into my life and be my Savior and my Lord."

I prayed, "Lord, thank You for letting us meet Lou tonight. I thank You that You have heard her prayer. You have come into her heart. Thank You for Your promise that You will never leave her nor forsake her and will be with her always."

Jackie, sniffling in the back seat, continued our prayer. "Lord, thank You that Lou has made the most important decision of her life tonight. If we never see her again, we will see her again in heaven."

When we finished praying, I asked, "Lou, where is Jesus Christ right now in relation to you?"

Smiling broadly, she said, "He's in my heart."

"That's right; and how do you know He's there?"

"Because I asked Him in, and I feel Him."

"Yes, and if the feelings would be gone in the morning, you would know He is still there because He promised He would come in, and He doesn't lie. Not only did He come in, but He has promised never to leave you nor forsake you. All those things that would have been up on the screen of your life are not there anymore, because Jesus forgave you. You have a 'clean screen,' a new beginning—and that's good news!"

"Yes, it is," she smiled. "This is wonderful . . . I'd like to get your address."

At the very moment we finished exchanging addresses, her husband opened the car door and said, "Let's go, the police are getting ready to lead us out of here."

After the 10 minutes the Lord gave us together, Lou left with the light of Christ shining in her eyes and on her countenance.

Jackie moved up to the front seat and said, "Ney, the whole atmosphere was full of love as you talked with Lou. It was as though the Lord set a moment of time aside, and just for that moment the flood wasn't here."

We marveled together over the Lord's perfect timing.

On that cold night of fear and death, in the midst of trauma, this dear lady discovered God's love for her.

The following Christmas, I received a small package containing two handmade crosses, one gold and one silver. In the package was a note from Lou saying, "One is for you, and one is for Jackie. Thank you for all you did to help me the night of the flood."

It seemed that my life would be forever divided with references to "before" and "after" the flood. It was after the flood that Marilyn Henderson shared with me something Jesus had said, "For whoever wishes to save his life shall lose it; and whoever loses his life for My sake and the gospel's shall save it."[5] I was familiar with the verse, but the part about "losing my life for the gospel's sake" stood out to me.

My life had been spared three times that night, getting out of the building before it was filled with water and mud to the ceiling, making it across the bridge before it was destroyed, and hearing the directions to get out of my car and up to higher ground. My life had been spared for a purpose.

I found the flood had caused me to think through in a new way Jesus Christ's command to go into all the world and preach the gospel.[6] In a deeper way I found myself saying, "Lord, for the rest of my life I want to give my life for the sake of the gospel. Use my life to help reach the world for You."

It is interesting to me that Jesus concluded His Sermon on the Mount by talking about a flood. He said,

> "Therefore every one who hears these words of Mine, and acts upon them, may be compared to a wise man, who built his house upon the rock. And the rain descended, and the floods came, and the winds blew, and burst against that house; and yet it did not fall, for it had been founded upon the rock. And every one who hears these words of Mine, and does not act upon them, will be like a foolish man, who built his house upon the sand. And the rain descended, and the floods came, and the winds blew, and burst against that house; and it fell, and great was its fall."[7]

If we act upon His Word, if we take God at His word, we will be wise, and our lives will be solidly set on the rock of His words. If we don't take Him at His word, we will be foolish, building our lives upon the sand.

Most of us will never go through a real flood, but we will all go through the "floods of life." While we are in our personal "floods," God wants us to take Him at His word, believing that what He says is truer than how we feel or any circumstance we will ever face, because:

HEAVEN AND EARTH WILL PASS AWAY
BEFORE HIS WORD PASSES AWAY

Notes

CHAPTER ONE

1. I Thessalonians 5:18 (KJV).
2. Romans 8:28.
3. Matthew 24:35.
4. Hebrews 13:15 (KJV).

CHAPTER THREE

1. Romans 1:17 (KJV).
2. I John 5:4.
3. Luke 7:7.
4. Luke 7:9.
5. Mark 4:40.
6. Matthew 24:35.
7. I Peter 1:25.
8. Isaiah 40:8.
9. Jeremiah 31:3.
10. Acts 10:34.
11. Romans 8:29.

CHAPTER FOUR

1. Matthew 24:12.
2. Acts 24:16.
3. I Timothy 1:18b-19.
4. Proverbs 21:5,6 (LB).

CHAPTER FIVE

1. I John 4:16.
2. Psalms 47:4.
3. Psalms 139:13.
4. Ephesians 3:14,15.
5. Ephesians 6:2,3.
6. Proverbs 1:8,9.

CHAPTER SIX

1. John 10:10a.
2. Luke 18:1 (KJV).
3. I Thessalonians 5:18 (KJV).
4. Romans 8:28.
5. I John 1:5.
6. Romans 8:29.
7. Galatians 5:22,23.
8. Psalms 133:1.

CHAPTER SEVEN

1. I John 4:4.
2. Matthew 6:9-14.
3. John 17:15.
4. Ephesians 6:10-17.
5. John 8:44.
6. Genesis 3:2.
7. Revelation 12:10.
8. Romans 8:1,31-34.
9. Romans 8:35-39.
10. Hebrews 13:5.
11. Isaiah 43:4.
12. Genesis 3:1-5.
13. Genesis 50:20.
14. John 11:21,32.
15. John 11:40.
16. II Timothy 2:25,26.
17. Matthew 17:20.
18. Ephesians 1:18-23.

CHAPTER EIGHT

1. Galatians 5:22,23.
2. Brother Lawrence, *The Practice*

of the Presence of God, Fleming
H. Revell Co., Old Tappan, New
Jersey, 1958, p. 16.
3. Matthew 6:25, 28-30.
4. Matthew 6:31-33.
5. Ephesians 3:20.
6. Matthew 6:34.

CHAPTER NINE

1. I Corinthians 3:6,7; Ephesians
   4:16.
2. Romans 5:1.
3. Romans 5:6-10.
4. John 15:9.
5. John 14:9.
6. Luke 22:31-34; Matthew 26:35.
7. Luke 22:54-62.
8. Mark 16:6,7.
9. Luke 23:34.
10. I Corinthians 13:5.
11. Psalms 103:12.
12. Jeremiah 31:34.
13. Miles J. Stanford, *Principles of
    Spiritual Growth*, Back to the
    Bible Broadcast, Lincoln, Nebras-
    ka, 1974, p. 31.
14. I John 4:18.
15. Philippians 2:13.
16. Psalms 138:8.

CHAPTER TEN

1. Romans 3:23.
2. Romans 6:23 (KJV).
3. John 14:6.
4. Revelation 3:20.
5. Mark 8:35.
6. Mark 16:15.
7. Matthew 7:24-27.